THE MEDIUMSHIP OF SPIRIT
The Ascension of William Alexander Oribello

William Alexander Oribello & Aurora Thyme

Global Communications

The Mediumship of Spirit

The Ascension of William Alexander Oribello

By William Alexander Oribello and Aurora Thyme

ISBN-10: 1606111515
ISBN-13: 978-1606111512

Published in the United States of America

Timothy Green Beckley: Editorial Director
Carol Rodriguez: Publishers Assistant
Cover Art: Tim Swartz

Published by:
Global Communications/Inner Light Publications
P.O. Box 753
New Brunswick, NJ 08903

DEDICATION

I would like to dedicate this book to my loyal followers who made it possible for my works to reach a larger audience all over the world. Without them, the Great Mysteries would forever remain hidden from mankind.

Of course this book would not have been possible without the loving help of my friend and student Aurora Thyme, who heard my voice calling from across infinity and answered without hesitation or doubt.

I would also like to thank my publisher, Timothy Green Beckley, of Inner Light Publications. His friendship and wisdom was an inspiration to me, and he has always been a source of encouragement and help in releasing my books.

I encourage all of you to look at the people in your lives and consider how much better you are for knowing and loving them, and being loved by them. For it is love alone that keeps us going and ultimately connects us with GOD the creator.

William Alexander Oribello

THE MEDIUMSHIP OF SPIRIT

Contents

A Word From The Publisher Timothy Green Beckley

AS many of his devoted students realize, Bill passed away quite a number of years ago now. He has been missed, but his work goes on. His books such as *Bible Spells, Godspells, Sacred Magic and Candle Burning with the Psalms* are more popular than ever before.

But the truth is, Rev Oribello is still with us and continues to assist on the earth plane, for in a sense he is NOT "gone," but resides alongside of us in another dimension. And he is still willing to offer a helping hand whenever possible.

This is the story of his "passing." But it is by no means a sad story. He is a story of everlasting life.

He lives and resides in our hearts and minds today. Welcome him from the otherside as he has much to offer.

THE MEDIUMSHIP OF SPIRIT

ONE: Life -The Great Mystery

IT is funny that one really never stops to consider what life is all about until it is over. When the physical body dies, and the spirit returns to its natural state of being, then the ways of the Universe become clear. Not everything is answered...there are still mysteries that await discovery, that is what makes life, all life, physical and spiritual, so interesting.

Life is the manifestation of the friction of the force of a spiritual entity upon a physical form through the Cosmic Life-giving Energy that permeates all. When the balance of the positive spiritual force and the negative material resistance is broken, disease is the result.

Everything vibrates from the tiny cell to the entire body of a plant, animal or of a man as well as the whole Universe. The most common cause of breaking the harmonious healthy vibrations of our body and its organs is the eating of foods and the drinking of liquids whose vibrations are very low or negative. All these substances are called toxic. Is it now plain to everyone why we advocate moderation from meat, cow's milk, white bread, white sugar, salt, tobacco and all other denatured foods as being toxic substances?

The same thing can be said when using plastic materials used as containers, plates, etc. or in synthetic clothing which; are toxic substances. The negative invisible vibrations emanated from these materials and unnatural substances penetrate our bodies and its organs and cells, and break the harmonious healthy life's rhythm in man and cause the multitude of diseases.

The only sure cure for the patient is to come back to the Natural way of living, to have faith in himself and in God, to exercise and be happy. Only, under these simple natural conditions all forces of Nature are then available for the restoration back to health of the sick and to keep him healthy as Nature intends her creatures to be.

We live in a time when it seems that so many people have forgotten their heritage, their roots back to Mother Earth. They have forgotten that their very existence is due to an extremely complex dance of factors that are necessary in order for life to arise.

THE MEDIUMSHIP OF SPIRIT

THE WORLD OF VIBRATIONS

Scientists and physicists have pondered for years on what reality is made of. They have come up with all sorts of interesting theories that result in heated arguments, hurt egos and plenty of bad Karma. However, the nature of reality is not so complicated and its inner workings have been available to those who take the time to quiet down for a while and listen to what creation is saying to them.

If scientists were truly interested in the truth, all they to do was consult the shaman, priests, and mystics who for centuries have been patiently explaining to their students what the world is made of: Everything in the universe is in the form of vibration.

Psychics and clairvoyants talked about vibrations long before the dissection of the atom. Indeed, in the long ago, they would persistently describe a person, place or thing or an event as a kind of "vibration." ("I see you in such-and-such vibration," meaning a place or condition. Or, "You will encounter a certain vibration . . ." Meaning a person or event they would say.) And this goes back to a time when science was still inclined to think of matter as composed of solid particles.

Now, thanks largely to theoretical physics, those fictitious building blocks of matter have been dissipated into a vast universal complex of vibrating energy patterns, thoroughly confirming the psychic terminology of the past. Moreover, we have learned to use vibrational power in practical ways that range from the pulsating electro-magnetic energy which powers the machines of industry to the waves of (hypothetically unpopular) ether which tantalize our vibrational awareness via radio, television and other methods.

Is there not, however, a more important clue to the nature of both the physical and metaphysical universe in the extraordinary preoccupation with vibration in present-day mechanics? We have radio waves, heat waves, light waves, ultra-violet rays, X-rays, gamma rays, etc. They are all the same vibrations—just shorter or longer in wave length or slower or faster in frequency, according to the classifications we have invented for them. . . . Except that our descriptive categories seem to be narrow and confining in terms of universal verities.

THE MEDIUMSHIP OF SPIRIT

Radio waves, for example, are a longer and less rapid version of light waves; X-rays and gamma rays are still shorter and higher in frequency, and so on up and down the vibrational scale. Yet the communicators through human instruments we call psychics or mediums keep talking about "finer" and "faster" or "higher" vibrations that are so far beyond the sensitive dials of our measuring devices they cannot be detected.

Is there any reason why these communicators should not be believed? There can only be a theoretical objection, and sound theory is not apt to suggest a priori, once and for all, that electro-magnetic vibrations suddenly come up against a blank wall and stop at a certain maximum or minimum wave length and frequency rate. There is no showing of either an upper or lower vibrational limit, except possibly in the periodicity terms of atomic particles considered without their "ghosts." Much of the evidence of psychical research, as well as trends in theoretical physics itself, seems to indicate that the construction of the atom may not be limited to one set of energy "quanta," or a single set of energy patterns of limited frequency range, but may encompass a broader range of wave lengths and frequencies limited only by infinity.

This may shock the theoretical and mathematical sensibilities of those devotees of Planck and modern wave mechanics who have conceived of certain limitations of frequency range within the wave packets of the atom. However, the quantum theory has come to be regarded more as a tool than a solution to atomic structure, and the "singularity," separateness, or apartness of particles has long since given way to the idea of indivisible wave packages without clear cut boundary lines. They are in some way inextricably bound to one another by neutral bridging zones and extensions 'round and about the wave bundles themselves.

This is quite in accord with the fundamental unity of the universe as taught by occultists. They speak, on one hand, of the indivisible, interlocking sets of vibrational patterns which constitute the nature of tangible forms and experience of the physical world and, on the other, of "planes" and "degrees" that are extensions of physical matter, concentric shells of consciousness and vibration that emanate from the physical world. These extensions, in turn, graduate farther and farther away, both in terms of consciousness and time-space, until they merge into cosmic and universal spheres approaching "infinite" being.

THE MEDIUMSHIP OF SPIRIT

Yet, at least within the orders of planes within their ken, they still speak of place and form as though these concepts continue to exist with tangible reality, even on the higher vibrational levels. It is a quantitative rather than a qualitative differentiation which is to be inferred from the very use of such terms as "degree" and "level," these being used to describe the ascending steps of vibration and conscious awareness. Both terms are employed for earth conditions (e.g., the Earth Plane), as well as for extraterrestrial (beyond earth) properties.

If there is form in all of these quantitative after-life degrees (except the near-infinite), then there are the corresponding elements of form, the same kind of nebulous building blocks we call atoms and molecules, as we find on the earth level, and they should therefore be subject to the same laws, the same vibrational constitution and the same indivisibility (lack of singularity) as physical matter. And the term "physical matter" no longer seems to be redundant, since we now can conceive of a kind of non-physical or quasi-physical matter in the higher vibrational worlds.

Now the "ghost" of the atom takes on a very real and unghostly significance. Physicists speak unreservedly of the atomic shells within which particle-packets of vibrating energy of a given value are confined. It is therefore conceivable that the atomic structure may also be composed of shells or degrees or planes of vibrating energy on ascending frequency levels. That is, there should, in view of the representation of "higher planes of vibration" by psychic communicators, be corresponding frequency levels within the atom itself.

ENERGY AND MOTION

The idea of higher, finer layers of energy motion within every physical body, every material object thus becomes more tenable, and the proposition of an infinite limit to such vibrational levels appears rational, whether we think of them in terms of quasi-physical structure or unfolding consciousness, and whether the vibrational patterns are continuous or progressively arranged in steps or quantum jumps.

Forms are declared by occultists to be composed of not only physical matter but "astral" or etheric doubles. And there are doubles of the doubles, counterpart forms in higher, finer vibrational steps that ascend toward an infinite state or into a realm of "universal consciousness." Meanwhile, from state to state, there is a kind of "bridge" which enables the ego-centered consciousness, under certain conditions, we are told, to travel between the levels. Therefore, it may be no coincidence that theoretical physics also speaks of a bridging property between the ill-defined energy states of matter.

The bridging therefore may also conceivably be between frequency levels which at least approach, in the end, the limit of infinity and so are finally rooted in what the metaphysician calls the Infinite Consciousness. (It is also referred to by such names as the "Absolute," the "Core of Light" and "Universal Consciousness.")

That there is a correspondence between the neutralized, bridging-binding stuff of the atom and the shell-like spheres spoken of in psychic communications is indicated by reports from these sources that discarnate entities can sometimes find themselves in dead zones between active planes where no life or activity exists and from which they may find difficulty in extracting themselves, that is, difficulty in gravitating without some discomfort to a level where activity does exist.

These zones could well be neutral layers between vibrational planes, and no doubt an astral counterpart of the neutron and the neutrino, at least the counterpart components of the neutron may exist there.

LIGHT AND INFINITY

It is significant that metaphysical sources continually make reference to infinity. The term is constantly reiterated, and the soul's cyclic progress toward an Infinite Source is emphasized in many teachings. The old axiom, "As above, so below," may well apply, physically and metaphysically.

If this is so, if vibrations can be rapid to the point of infinity or, conversely, so infinitely slow as to approach a point of complete rest, might not this require some overhauling of our ideas of space and matter?

In the first place, there may be some new support for the idea that there is not only a time dimension in the universe but an "eternity" (infinity) dimension as well. It would seem that mathematical physicists and cosmologists should be able to do much with this broad view of a total universe of infinitely varied vibrational systems.

Evidences of both the corpuscular and vibrational nature of light may likewise fall into a completely coherent scheme when the total, all inclusive nature of vibration is understood. And in philosophy the ancient concept of an "Absolute" takes on new significance. Secondly, the reliability of one of the most sacred constants known to science, the velocity of visible light in a vacuum, may come into question as a part of this understanding.

Since light, with a velocity of 186,000 plus miles per second, represents only one small segment of the potentially infinite spectrum, is this constant as real as it has been regarded? Is it reliable on the earth-plane, much less on the super-physical planes? And does it represent, as we have supposed, the maximum velocity attainable in the universe?

We may also ask: if light has a specific velocity, does all light have the same velocity? We say that light travels at a specified velocity, but what kind of light? No doubt it would be most difficult to show that infra-red and ultra-violet rays travel at different speeds, but may it not nevertheless be so, no matter how infinitesimal the variation, and what of more widely separated bands of the electro-magnetic spectrum?

HIGHER SPHERES

Communicators — teachers from what are often referred to as the "higher spheres," have spoken of traveling millions of miles in "a twinkling of an eye." They say this is done by means of a "shaft of light," a ray or higher octave of visible light which they project before themselves. They do not say this transfer is instantaneous or that it is merely a change in consciousness alone, although that is involved too.

They imply, in connection with a change of consciousness, some kind of transfer at high velocity from condition to condition and place to place, across a measurable distance in terms of the material aspect of the universe. They also report a lapse of time in this process, a calculable interval, no matter how short. They have said specifically in my presence that they travel at speeds greater than that of light.

THE MEDIUMSHIP OF SPIRIT

How is this possible? It would not be possible if we continued to insist that nothing is faster than visible light. It could be theoretically possible if we stop conceiving of light velocity as an irrevocable constant and start considering the likelihood of a third variable in electromagnetic radiation, the other two being wave length and frequency.

What the messages from "higher spheres" seem to intimate is that the velocity of vibrations also varies, directly according to frequency and inversely according to wave length, the higher the frequency, the faster the transmission of the vibration and the shorter the wave length. All vibration, it then appears, is not disseminated nor does it travel as a ray of the velocity of visible light but at speeds commensurate with frequency. Thus the shaft of invisible light, the "higher vibration," which enables an etheric messenger, as he says, to travel faster than visible light becomes theoretically comprehensible because, as he also says, he is truly operating in that "higher vibration."

He can therefore propel himself, in whatever appropriate spirit body we may specify, at speeds commensurate with incredibly high frequencies. It would be interesting to correlate the mathematical progressions inherent in the idea of variable velocity with an interpretation of the neutral zones found in the atom and reported in the super-physical realms.

Would frequencies traveling at different rates cancel each other out at certain points, accounting for the whole atomic and cosmic plan of active and inactive energy layers and shells? And could the failure to recognize a third variable have been a stumbling block in the way of a perfected unified field theory? Once that naughty constant is transformed into a more universally applicable variable, with the total range of electro-magnetic vibrational systems under consideration, may we not then be equipped to wrestle with a more universal formula? Is this something that God the Creator even allows us to understand?

With this step, we may also unlock yet another door, alluded to above. There has been much talk in recent years, even among scientists, about something called the "ghost" of the atom.

Psychic communicators have been telling us from the time of the Fox sisters that they live in a real world of places, people and things and that in their worlds they "vibrate" on different levels of consciousness; as one speaker through a medium once tried to explain it: "We go at a faster speed than you do."

Another amplified by saying that the word "go" not only applied to travel from consciousness to consciousness but also to the very process of existence in the environment of higher vibrations. He put it in this way: "We vibrate faster than you do."

He then assured us that in his world, invisible to us because of the difference in rates of vibration, there were buildings, flowers, trees, people with bodies and clothing and varied activities reminiscent of the Earth level of "consciousness." Let me assure you, these things are true. The world of the spirit is intertwined with the physical world; As on Earth, so too in Heaven.

BUILDING BLOCKS

There are stated differences between the physical and supra-physical worlds, of course, but they are not important to this discussion. However, it is in the above-worlds that we may look for satisfying clues to the "ghost" of the atom. For if there are objects, places and forms in the so-called etheric worlds, then there must also be molecules and atoms, vibrational building blocks on higher frequency levels. These should be quite similar in structure to those we seek to analyze on the earth level.

The earthly building blocks, now to be regarded as totally vibrational and non-singular in character, are composed of bundles of pulsating energy we have identified as electrons, protons and other microcosmic quasi-particles, including neutral combinations which may or may not be finally related to an infinity dimension.

These strictly vibrational components of the atom thus are to be recognized as not at all uniquely associated with one level of frequencies but, instead, arranged in a sequence of frequency levels. The progression would correspond precisely with the vibrational environment of the invisible spheres, planes, zones and degrees we hear so much about in psychic communications (and exchanges of energy may well accord completely with Planck's law).

THE MEDIUMSHIP OF SPIRIT

In other words, when we speak of the astral replica of a physical body or the etheric archetype of a material object, common parlance in the metaphysical field, we are merely referring to patterns of energy vibrating at higher rates; that is, frequency rates which correspond with the ascending "etheric" levels and progress on toward infinity. And again we can see that the occultist may be right when he asserts that every atom, every particle, and every wave has its roots firmly planted in the Infinite Source.

If each atom has as yet undetected levels of "higher" vibration —i.e., an atomic astral body or ghost or a progressive series of such concentric wave levels, we can understand (1) how an object can be destroyed and yet leave an etheric trace or replica; (2) how physical bodies can be maintained co-existent with etheric or "spirit" bodies and (3) how these spirit bodies can have physical aspects in an environment of "higher vibration" above, beyond and ultimately independent of the gross lower frequencies of the earthly vibration.

In this connection, it is interesting to remember that many primitive peoples, including tribes of the North American Indians, have had the belief that inanimate objects possess etheric counterparts, an invisible substantiality which can be carried into the spirit life. This is the basis of the idea that weapons, implements, jewelry and even clothing buried with the deceased can be utilized in the spiritual spheres by means of their higher essence or double.

In short, it should be apparent that modern concepts of atomic theory can give some support to this primitive belief. Moreover, there is corroboration for the whole idea of a real, substantial and objective afterlife world (or series of worlds), which is a kind of double for the earth world and in which the astral doubles belonging to living beings freed from their earthly shells can move and have continued being.

Bodies composed of compatible vibrational complexes become solid and tangible to beings attuned to the same general frequency and invisible and intangible to those environmental vibrations or frequency levels which are markedly incompatible. Thus is the phenomenon of ghostly experiences better explained, such as a form which appears to pass through a solid wall or appears and disappears in a closed room. The temporary encasement of invisible etheric forms in ectoplasmic matter during materialization phenomena likewise can be better understood.

ETHERIC FORMS

The patterns of frequencies which make up a material form coexist with etheric forms attuned to higher vibrational levels, just as surely as the various radio frequencies we translate into sound and sight via our receivers can coexist with each other and with the vibrations of earth matter without interference. The problem of discrete planes and levels of vibration, as opposed to continuous frequencies without finite break, also may be resolved on the basis of atomic theory. Communicators generally agree that there are just such definitive spheres, shells or dimensions of vibration surrounding the earth and, as we have said, repeatedly refer to the "higher spheres" of vibration as though they were rational divisions, rather than mere literary allusions.

The emission and absorption of energy in relation to steps and jumps would seem to be in accord with the occult symbolism of "Jacob's Ladder," corresponding to the decrees of definitive energy levels. These are the divisions and planes referred to by communicators, who often identify them by name (e.g., the "astral plane") and number (the "seventh degree" or the "third sphere").

It but remains, in working out a coherent theory of etheric or spiritualistic counterparts within the atom, to envision levels of frequency within the atomic structure corresponding to the levels of vibration of the cosmic structure. Not only would we then regard the atom as composed of wave packets orbiting and absorbing or emitting specific quanta of energy according to formula but likewise as coexistent bundles of "higher energy," higher frequency levels, that would still preserve the "essence" (and this is another ancient metaphysical word which begins to come into focus) of form on many such levels. In other words, form is a many-layered thing, each layer being a vibrational complex within certain frequency limits.

Again, vibration is the clue to the phenomena of physical medium-ship. The materialization can be considered to be a process of condensation (another term often employed in the séance room) of vibrations originating in the supra-physical environments. Earth energies are drawn as needed (and as often stated) from medium and sitters to clothe the etheric manifestations and bring them into temporary visibility. The precipitated visible forms, however, are vibrationally unstable in most cases, though not all, and are incapable of permanent solidification.

That these temporarily material forms are subject to will, mental activity, merely points up the part which directed consciousness plays in the whole cosmic scheme of vibrational activity. Studies of thought forms created in the supra-physical atmosphere of an individual likewise are significant to the whole problem, as are losses of energy (typical cold winds and chilly physical reactions) common in ghostly phenomena. Power for physical manifestations, it is said, often is drawn from immediate surroundings, accounting for a sudden loss of heat.

In the long view, we may do well to agree with a clairvoyant's picture of matter: atoms and bodies of atoms composed of "wheels within wheels," turning ever faster on each step toward infinite movement. Or as one clairvoyant expressed it: "I can see myself rising from plane to plane, from different reality to different reality, each more real, more alive than the last, shedding bodily coatings as I go, until I finally approach a great sun, the Infinite Source of all." Another expressed the concept of enfolding bodies by comparing it to a folding telescope that reaches into space toward a faraway source of light and then, when not in use, is collapsed into a compact package, with the extensions still self-contained.

FREQUENCY LEVELS

Conversely, an entity descending toward the physical level would unfold layers of condensation, like the opening of a folding telescope from the source-of-light end, with the far end still rooted in the dimensions of immensity. More accurately, perhaps, every object and body could be visualized as having their counterparts on many frequency levels, like images reflected from one looking glass into another and reverse, trailing off apparently forever into a misty realm of infinite duplications.

We are told that mental activity and consciousness itself are the prime movers of the vibrational qualities of form. Metaphysical teachers under many names and through various channels, mediumistic and otherwise, have long emphasized this idea. The great universal Prime Mover is said to have blown upon the unmoved waters of the cosmic sea of unexpressed consciousness to give objective expression to Himself. The Mover's breath having created ripples in the sea, the worlds of form were born. The rippling waves then become increasingly complex with rhythmic cycles on many levels of the cosmic deep, but within each configuration of undulating wave forms, the living breath of the Great Consciousness continues to be the mover. Hence, within each form is implanted the universal urge to reflect, represent and express the true form or formlessness of the Creator.

Each individual, in whatever form, is an expression of the Creator within the depths of the Universal Consciousness as a result of the great initial breath of life. Therefore, it is said that the perfection of the individual depends upon how well he expresses the Infinite Consciousness. And so, once again, we have the approach to infinity in both physical and metaphysical terms.

The individual, although inseparable from all other consciousness, nevertheless moves and is moved according to a particular state or level of consciousness. Each attracts and is attracted to an appropriate vibrational environment governed by the development and evolution of expanding consciousness. This, then, we are told, is the role of each unfolding unit of Infinite Consciousness as it tries to achieve total objective, as well as subjective, consciousness in the vibrational worlds of form.

Each gravitates to the level of expression appropriate to his level of consciousness and his evolutionary development. So these various dimensions of vibrational frequency are also properly referred to as planes of consciousness. There is the earth plane, the astral plane (with many varying zones and degrees); there are other spiritual planes, spiritual and cosmic spheres and finally a potential state of universal perception we may call "infinite awareness."

Here it should also be remembered that there is general agreement among those who have brought forth "revealed" teachings in various ages that the process of evolution and development of conscious awareness is not entirely automatic. There is a certain impetus toward a certain end result (namely, infinite awareness), but the variety of experience and the non-duplication of the cyclic paths of individual expression are occasioned by an important consideration: Each individual expression of the Great Creator has within itself the Father's creative urge.

So, being also a creator, it attempts individually and uniquely to manipulate the forces and forms of objective creation according to the state of conscious awareness and realization that has unfolded. It seeks ever to create the one true expression of the Master Self, the Master Builder of form that will most truly interpret, represent and reflect the infinitely inexpressible and ineffable Source, the ultimate Archetype. This, of course, is the free will aspect of the cosmic picture.

Implicit within the confines of a world of forms, however, are certain limitations. For instance, there are not only environmental limitations of individual expression on the physical plane but in other spheres as well.

After passing from the physical body, the individual automatically gravitates to the vibrational level appropriate to his own "vibration" and consciousness; nor is he yet through with phenomena, the struggle for expression through physical type forms. He is still governed by a world of energies. In fact, psychic communicators often speak of "energy patterns" and "power" in connection with tangible experiences in the post-physical dimensions. Furthermore, the word "gravitate" (to gravitate from vibration to vibration or plane to plane) is also theirs.

Unfortunately, though we encounter gravity during every moment of our earthly experience and are evidently faced with gravitational problems on the super-physical levels, scientists are undecided as to what gravity really is. There are numerous hypotheses but no widely accepted theory. We just don't know, in the terms of modern astrophysics, the precise nature of gravity. The laws of Newton are of some help in gauging the phenomena but of little assistance in explaining the phenomena. Einstein's amendments to the Newtonian laws furnish a more universal meaning, but the answer is not yet complete.

No one, least of all the present writer, should pretend that the complete answer lies within the scope of a single formula, a simple theoretical solution or any one uncomplicated discovery just over the scientific horizon. Rather, the problem is so fundamental to the total explanation of the universe that a complete understanding, it seems, would carry with it answers to all of the mysteries of life and matter.

THE MEDIUMSHIP OF SPIRIT

NEW DIRECTIONS

Nevertheless, as there have been and must continue to be, as a part of the evolution of consciousness, sporadic step-by-step approaches to full understanding, we are justified in seeking for new directions which may point the way. We have indicated that extrasensory sources have often been of value in the past. So, for whatever it is worth, the writer herewith relates her own experience with spirit inspiration.

We have noted that ideas sometimes seem to come from internal and external sources beyond the conscious mind. In the present instance, I had been reading about some of the hypotheses advanced to account for the phenomena of gravitation when I was impelled to write down a number of impressions. Actually, these were more than impressions; they came into my consciousness as compelling thoughts, as though dictated to me. In fact, I can say they were transmitted word by word, so clearly and without break that I was required to write rapidly to get them on paper before the phrases faded.

This is precisely what I received:

"Gravity is a function of motion and, by extension, of vibration. Since everything is in a state of vibration, gravity then is a function of the rate of vibration. Why, therefore, do all bodies of the same frequency pattern attract each other according to Newton's law?

"For the answer, it is necessary to visualize matter, not as solid objects, but as levels of vibration, with these levels interlocking in such a manner and according to a mathematical order as will require their mutual assistance in maintaining equilibrium.

"Gravity is then seen to be the force which preserves the universe in a state of equilibrium by means of vibration; or, again by extension, through the Divine Consciousness or the Divine Will. Since everything is also consciousness, gravity is a function of the state of consciousness or a function of Universal Consciousness or Divine Will.

"Everything being an expression of that Will or Consciousness, gravity expresses it also. How does it work?

"Not so much by a force of attraction as by a pressure of interlocking motion and vibration which prevents the universe from flying apart. The universe is a unit, and all sections of that unit interlock and interact according to the rate of vibration and the state of consciousness that is determined by the state of evolution of cosmic and individual consciousness.

"Hence, everything is a direct function of the Divine Will or the Power of Creation."

It has occurred to me that a universe in equilibrium, one which does not fly apart, seems to clash paradoxically with the observed phenomena of the expanding heavens; that is, the galactic clusters which seem to be flying apart at a tremendous rate. The answer impressed upon me seems simple enough and in accordance with the cyclic nature of all things.

Motion and vibration, action and reaction, must ever be cyclic. It is erroneous to consider one motion or set of motions in a given cycle as irreversible or as conclusive evidence of what happens in a total eternity dimension. Specifically, it may be said that the expanding universe just is not always expanding. There are phases (a term used both in its technical and literary sense), and the observed phase may be only one segment of the complete cycle.

Some communicators from psychic sources have said that the heavenly bodies, such as planets and suns, burst forth periodically from a central source, then fly apart until, "like soap bubbles," they burst (disintegrate) one by one. The process is repeated on a grand scale after a long coalescing process that again brings about necessary conditions for a new explosion. This, incidentally, is not inconsistent with some current cosmological speculations.

All of this does not firmly bridge the gap between physics and metaphysics or join the schism between science and religion. Yet it may have some value as an exercise, an indication of the possibilities of some greater depth perception into dimensions we have tended to ignore.

More psychic hints and hunches than have been dreamed of in our philosophy may assuredly be expected in this space age of incredible discovery. A strange admixture of material experiment and infinite insight may yet produce the Philosopher's Stone to give us many nuggets of Golden Truths from the dross of technological advancements.

By creating a vision of your desired state and putting energy into it regularly, you use mind power to shape the very stuff of creation. You create this imagined "reality" in your mind to the point where your subconscious actually believes it to be physical reality and goes about making it so. It will attract the circumstances, the people, and the opportunities you need to bring about the vision you have created.

If you are doubtful about this, consider for a moment that you are doing this anyway. The only difference is that you may be unaware you are doing it. If so, your overall vibration is incoherent, and hence your results fluctuate wildly. By becoming conscious, you take conscious control of the creative process and can learn to manifest at will.

Another way to change your vibration rate is to act "as if." If you had already attained what you seek, how would you think and act? Well, start thinking and acting that way right now. Again, this helps to impress the dominant vibration you choose upon your subconscious mind. Again, you have been doing this all your life anyway. Simply take conscious deliberate control of the process from now on.

Taking time to meditate regularly on the truth that all is vibration, seeing this reality in all is myriad guises, will also help reinforce it upon your mind – both conscious and subconscious. You will begin to believe it, and what you believe is what you act upon.

We may measure and bridge the divisions of the universe to our heart's content, but in the end it will be immeasurable consciousness and insight that will produce satisfying answers to the mysteries.

TWO: Returning Home

I stood on the edge, between two worlds; one foot forwards, one foot back. Behind me was my physical life, the material world. It was familiar and there was still much I had not completed. Now my old body was fading, its heart slowing down, its energies waning. It was tired and finally ready to give itself back to the dust from which it had come.

In front of me was the world of spirit. The fountain from which all life had sprung, spraying throughout the multiples of Universes, seeking fertile ground to grow and prosper. It beckoned to me with the promise of fresh starts, reunions with old friends, soothing hands for the pains that I carried with me; and love, unconditional love.

I looked back, everyone does. How would the world get along without me? How would I get along without the world? I would miss so much, the smell of fresh sea air on a quiet sunny morning, the sound of birds as they sang of their love of life and the freedoms of the sky. The embrace of a child, fresh and ready for what life has in store. The simple pleasures of hot chocolate on a cold day, or laughing the afternoon away with those you care about the most. How could I leave this all behind?

We continually obsess with all that is wrong with the world; the hunger, sickness, wars, man's inhumanity to man. We tear ourselves apart looking for those small differences in which to attach our hate and bigotry upon. We blind ourselves with watching for signs when God will decide that enough is enough and sends Gabriel to blow the horn of eternity.

We love to hate, and hate to love.

Worst of all, we fail to see just how beautiful the world really is. We miss the good by concentrating on the evil. We forget to say "I love You" because we are always looking for ways to push each other away. I turn from what used to be and take that one giant step forwards, to what will be, to my future. One part of my life is over – another has just begun.

THREE: To Your Good Health

HEALTH is yours for free, if you will but obey natural laws, eat only live, health-giving foods and think only positive, cheerful thoughts. Yes you can switch to positive thoughts once you realize these are what make for health, happiness and success in life. It IS true that you are what you eat as it is that you are headed in the direction your habitual thoughts lead you, to ease or disease.

Malnutrition in the land of plenty is a paradox of life. Overeating has become one of our devastating and disease producing habits. However, because the wrong foods are eaten, along with the fact that our soil no longer contains the life-giving minerals and other nutriments vitally needed to maintain normal blood and body tissue, malnutrition has become one of our commonest occurrences despite our overeating.

To add to our depleted vitality, most of the grains today are devitalized though they are labeled "enriched" as we find in white flour products, bread, macaroni and other pastes and rich pastries. Most bread is no longer our staff of life but rather a dead weight. Equally devastating is the free use of chemical poisons used as fertilizers and sprays.

Nature is continually active to keep the body in perfect health by removing waste matter through the skin, lungs, kidneys, bowels and mucous membranes. But Nature's efforts can be thwarted by the basic cause of all disease: food deficiencies or excesses and unnatural ways of living, causing nerve power depletion and resultant suppression of all secretions and excretions.

The latter causes the retention and accumulation of poisons, wastes and toxins in the body, the condition being known as toxemia. The body makes an extra effort to expel the poisons by way of simple illness; colds, fever, rashes and diarrhea. Fresh air, sunshine, pure water, exercise, proper food, rest, these simple requirements are all that are necessary for proper functioning of the entire system resulting in good health. You will be surprised how good you feel by following these simple steps.

Colitis and irritable-bowel-syndrome is merely an advanced form of catarrh. Catarrh is a result of the over-use of sugars and artificially sweetened and refined starchy foods. Lack of the B-complex factors is one of the causes of this malnutritional condition. You may be constantly eating and yet starving slowly to death over a period of years. To stop this, you should stop taking laxatives and cathartics and start eating properly. Stay away from white flour, get outdoors frequently, get away from people who are disturbing. Seek Nature and follow natural law.

When Nature calls, you need to permit everything else to be secondary. Constipation is usually the result of not answering Nature's call promptly. Learn to relax, to eat slowly, to laugh and smile and play. Take an interest in others. Irritable-bowel-syndrome will vanish. Once again you will be healthy and young and eager participant for this very special thing called life.

The diet of all rheumatics is universal, they are heavy meat eaters, eat white flour products, too many sugars and starches and lack the proper body building minerals. All these produce an acid condition called autointoxication, toxicity or toxemia – in other words, a poison-filled system.

To reverse the process, start the day with a glass of water that you have squeezed the juice of a lemon. Follow that with an additional glass of water. Take a few bending exercises to relieve the stiffness of your joints and muscles, and lazily stretch the arms, legs and spine as the family cat does

Fruit, an egg or two, soft-boiled, and 100-percent whole wheat toast or rolled oats or other whole grain cooked cereal make a good breakfast Replace sugar with honey and don't use any more sweets for two weeks or a month. Eat more fruits, steamed vegetables and green tossed salads.

Lean meats, eggs, fresh fruits, vegetables and nuts are all good foods. Following this simple regimen you'll soon notice a great improvement in your health it can cure your headaches, improve your eyesight and stop your rheumatic aches. When eliminating acid forming foods, you naturally eliminate the suffering they cause.

The so-called acid fruits have a final alkaline reaction in the stomach, as do nearly all fruits and vegetables. To be healthy there should be an alkaline reserve in the body Hurry, worry, fear, grief, distress, and excitement all charge the body with acid. To balance this condition, build up your alkaline reserve and keep well. After a month of eating live foods you will have formed, along with good health, good eating habits. Continue eating simple foods and you will learn the joys of a zesty appetite, satisfying meals and exuberant health.

The four great students of health, pioneers in the field of Natural Therapy were Bernarr Macfadden, Dr. Benedict Lust, Dr. Henry Lindlahr, and Dr. Frederick W. Collins. These great advocates of natural living all believed that the lymphatic stream had much to do with disease. Retained and accumulated morbid matter upsets the lymphatic system, they said. Stagnation follows causing poor circulation and the blood stream becomes affected; tiredness, irritation and fatigue, colorless skin, flaccid tissue and general debility results. This is auto-intoxication followed by a state of catarrh in an attempt of the body to cleanse and purify itself.

Most medical men are agreed that toxicity permits, feeds and propagates diseases and that detoxification of the human body cures disease, restoring the body to vital health.

There are many ways known to detoxify the human system, but the cure is too simple, by detoxifying the system. The cause of many diseases is toxicity of the blood, when you remove the obstructions and impediments in the body through eating proper foods, getting sufficient exercise and sunshine, then the natural healing function is freed to assert itself.

Self-preservation is Nature's first law, manifesting from the moment of birth and will fight against tremendous odds to keep life and health in the body. Given half a chance, it does the work you prepare the way by ridding the system of accumulated wastes. No matter what your illness, you can detoxify your system by going on a fruit, vegetable and pure water diet for three months more or less. In such a cleansed system, no germs can live. Your doctor knows this as it is part of his study at medical college. It is as simple as that. If you really want health with a capital "H", you can have it.

There are other cures such as the grape juice, carrot juice and other juices. All work to rid the body of poisons and allow Nature to rebuild the health.

Soybeans are a definite combater of heart disease. It is known for its high protein contents, is a native of China and is one of the oldest crops grown by man. Protein foods contain nitrogen, oxygen and sulfur which are strong acid dissolvers, hence good for any ailment and keep you in health

The yield of protein from soybeans, weight for weight is approximately twice that of meat; four times that of eggs, wheat and other cereals; five or six times that of bread; twice that of lima and navy beans, walnuts and most other nuts, and twelve times that of milk. This high protein content goes a long way to dissolving the acids in the system. Not only is heart disease is aided in this manner but all bodily discomforts.

The use of the soybean in place of meat, milk and eggs has the advantages of providing an oil that is free of cholesterol and soybean oil is rich in unsaturated, essential fatty acids, as well as being rich in lecithin and sitosterol. The high alkalinity of the soybean exerts a sparing action on the protein requirement of the body. A high protein soybean diet will not produce any harmful effects on the kidneys, and it is free from nucleoproteins. All of these reasons tell why soybeans are so good for you.

Here is another natural way to heal yourself and keep in health: eat garlic. Garlic, like other members of its family: onions, leeks and chives offer an excellent source of Vitamin C, and a fair amount of Vitamin A-B and G. It abounds in minerals of sulfur, iron and calcium and should be considered a most valuable medicinal, both as a preventative against possible disease, and as a curative when needed

Daily doses of garlic will help to fight disease of the nose and respiratory tract. Your Grandma would give you garlic for a cold, this was good advice. It has been recommended for persons with high blood pressure as an asthma remedy and to reduce bad cholesterol and produce good cholesterol. Moreover, garlic is an excellent intestinal antiseptic and an especially good stimulant to the digestive system.

A healthy life starts first and foremost with acceptance and love for self. We are all very complex beings and are a product of what we think, feel, focus our attention on, take into our bodies and bring with us on a soul level.

In any discussion of healthy lifestyles, we should remember that our thoughts and feelings are often the primary directors in how we feel and choose to live our lives. To have positive thoughts and harmonious feelings allows one to make lifestyle, exercise and dietary choices that energize the body and enliven the mind and spirit.

The first step begins when we acknowledge our intent to live a more positive and healthy life. Our willingness to let go of old habits sets the process in motion. The next step is to educate ourselves with the highest wisdom we can find on the subject and then put it into practical application to experience the benefits. It is important to discern clearly what information is presented to you and whether or not it rings a note of truth. If it sounds too good to be true or implies wonderful results with little effort, be cautious. Today's health fad can be tomorrow's illness.

When faced with change, we often feel that we have to give up something in order to embrace what is new. Although this is part of the process of letting go, it is also helpful to recognize we get so much more from the new experiences that it is worth the effort to change. We are actually embracing a new reality of greater balance and quality of life.

If we approach change with love we can decide to make a lifestyle change and in doing so we set up a permanent and sustainable way of living. In other words, when we love ourselves enough to let go of old, unhealthy habits and allow new ones to form, we benefit with better health and well being for all!

The amazing thing about our body is that it goes to health unless impeded – if you cut your finger the body heals, get a cold, your body heals. The body is designed to be youthful and healthy. It is only stress that ages the body and stress can be triggered by our thoughts, feelings, food, drugs, smoke, negative relationships, and the like.

Find ways to exercise the mind and body and you will be amazed at the vitality and energy you will have. What we put in the body can sustain us or hinder us. For example, many of us retain the eating habits of our youth – a time when we are active and growing physically. Yet, in later years we consume much greater quantities of food than our bodies truly require. This is born out of routine rather than physical need. Additionally, poor eating habits from early years often stick with us and can cause greater difficulties in later years if not corrected and updated. This is only one of the challenges we face with personal nutrition today.

THE MEDIUMSHIP OF SPIRIT

In these wonderful days of choice, it is becoming increasingly clear we need to practice discrimination in what we eat. It is not that any one item is bad or wrong; rather it is the cumulative effect that begins to stress and wear down the body. This, in turn, can make it difficult to maintain a positive attitude in life.

With lower energy we lose our balanced point of power. This can then affect our thoughts, feelings, relationships, career, etc. The cycle usually comes full circle with more improper eating to offset the negative feeling. Ironically, the solution may be easier than we think. The key is our willingness to change. We can begin by balancing our thoughts and feelings which leads us to a balanced physical body.

The best diet (or way of eating) is the one that is right for you, just like the best exercise is the one that you will actually do. We recognize the body requires fresh air, fresh water, fresh fruits and vegetables, mental stimulation and gentle exercise. In an organic and balanced approach, this brings the greatest harmony and sustains life naturally.

The body by itself does not specifically need drugs, tobacco, alcohol, meat, fish, eggs, dairy products, processed foods or refined sugar, salt, refined carbohydrates or refined fats. These are not good or bad items; rather, it is recognition that a balanced body does not require these things to sustain life. Many of these items are brought through conditioning, habit, and recreational experiences. Surprisingly, the body can handle these items, yet with a cost to efficiency, longevity and quality of life.

Obviously such a list is contrary to most current traditions and approaches and may sound rather harsh to some and boring to others. Yet when embraced, people find the greatest benefit with eating habits that provide the body with the most natural and simple ingredients.

Practically speaking, most people are not physically, emotionally, mentally or spiritually ready to take on drastic eating change. What is suggested is to become aware of what you eat, when you eat it and how it affects you. Take steps that are right for you. If you are a meat eater, you may choose to let go of red meat (or meat altogether) for a time to experiment. A vegetarian may choose to release other animal products like eggs or cheese to see how that affects them. Your body knows what is best for you and will help you if you listen.

THE MEDIUMSHIP OF SPIRIT

When we pursue a healthy lifestyle, we open ourselves to a vast universe of information. There is great wisdom around us along with many old, worn and outdated beliefs.

Love is a process of unfolding ourselves in all ways. A healthy lifestyle provides a better vehicle for our adventure. With a little patience, perseverance, and soul searching, we can enhance our life experience in delightful ways. Willingness to go within and question our current habits and beliefs is where we begin. It is not always easy, yet we can allow our inner guidance to show us how to bring about a healthier approach and understanding to life.

For example, let's take a look at our natural and innate experience about food sources. Humanity will naturally go out to a field, remove an apple from a tree, and bite into it. Yet we do not have the same inherent desire to run up to a living animal in a pasture, bite into and eat it while it is alive. In fact, such an image would repulse most people. This is an instinctive reaction to a deeper truth of our spiritual connection with all life.

In a similar regard, we find the logical use of pesticides, chemicals and hormones as a way to increase and sustain the yield of our crops and enhance the return and health of our livestock. Yet which of us would readily reach out and ingest the raw chemical, preservative, pesticide, or hormone if it were placed in a bottle or container before us? Our natural heart-felt reaction is to not use such artificial substances. However, we take these items in every day through our food.

The intent to improve our capacity to feed our selves and all others is noble and correct. When logic is combined with wisdom and love, we naturally find alternatives that are organic and sustainable on all levels and with harm to none.

The real key to healthful living and eating is "everything in moderation." There is nothing wrong with having the occasional hamburger, pizza or can of beer. But, if this is all that you eat everyday, then your body will soon start to rebel with all sorts of maladies.

Many of our modern health problems can be directly attributed to eating too much of the wrong things. Too much meat, too much fat, too much salt, sugar and refined grains; if you want to live a healthier life, then eat a lot more fruits and vegetables and a lot less of processed foods.

These are just a few examples of the many ways in which we can rethink and adjust our perspectives and create a happier and healthier experience on all levels. So, embrace what works for you and enjoy the journey.

Know that you can eat your way back to health, and live a much longer, healthier and happier life just as God the Creator intended.

FOUR: Leaving It All Behind

THE choice had been made, the silver cord had been severed and the final breath had been taken and released. I was now free to fly higher than the stars in the heavens, beyond the confines of the material senses. In this new world we are all one; we are beyond time; we are immortal; we are all joined together. We are love, and we are a part of God.

But, still, there is doubt.

It clouds my mind and keeps me tied to the world of pain and suffering. It is like a heavy coat that drags me down into cold, dark water; away from the light, away from freedom, away from my destiny.

I thought that I had been prepared for this doubt, prepared for the fear. But despite my best efforts, it was still there, gnawing at my soul with past sins, past unhappiness. Hurt that had been cast on me, and hurt that I had cast onto others.

It wrapped me so solidly, so completely, that I was encased in a cocoon of sensation. Pain, fear, jealousies, desires – all clung to me like thistles clinging to the fur of a dog. Forever entwined with no hope of removal and no hope of redemption.

I felt helpless, alone.

Yet, deep within, there was a glimmer.

Hope.

It started as a lone candle at the end of a dark hallway.

Distant, flickering. But it grew steadier.

It grew brighter. Finally, it engulfed me. It consumed me.

It burned away the doubt. It burned away the fear and pain.

In its place it offered hope, forgiveness.

It offered love.

FIVE: Make Your Wishes Come True

WHAT we think, our beliefs, how we see ourselves and our world, form the framework of our reality. Our world behaves just as we expect it to – as we think it will. And we get from it what we think we deserve.

Those of us, who believe we have bad luck, are victims of the circumstances of our lives, are pawns of an uncaring, unfeeling god, and will find that bad luck will continuously follow them throughout their lives.

Every time progress is made, they will find something waiting around the corner to steal what they worked so hard to get. This happens because that is what they expect to happen. That is what they believe will be waiting for them.

On the other hand, when you realize that you are responsible for the life you have created, that you created it through your thoughts, feelings and actions — through what you believe about yourself and the world — through the fear and love you generate within and around you, you begin to discover just how much power you have to get what you want out of life.

Changing beliefs, letting go of negative thoughts and adopting a more positive "yes, I can" attitude based on beliefs that are nurturing and loving can literally make the difference between happiness and sadness, success and failure.

Today there are thousands of books on the nature of reality, consciousness, positive thinking, all written with one primary objective: to expose the conflicts in our old belief systems and provide us with new frameworks, new attitudes that affirm rather than deny our power and release us to the life of love, good health, abundance and ease that is our natural birthright.

Yet, at the end of the day, changing your beliefs is as easy as changing your shirt. Once you decide you can, you will. As long as you believe you cannot, you are stuck. This shows the power in our beliefs about ourselves.

Words have vibrational frequency; just as colors and numbers can be associated with a vibrational frequency, so can sounds and words. Every letter of the alphabet can be associated with a number and every number, and every color, can be associated with a musical note. When letters are strung together to form a specific sound or word, the word is "charged" in a sense, with a specific frequency that is more than the sum of its parts, and that word then, influences all who think, read, speak or hear it.

Words are even further charged as humans attach certain emotions to specific words. The bible says "In the beginning was the word," inferring that the universe, all of God's creation was created from some spoken expression, a Godly sound.

So what kind of Godly sounds are you creating day by day? And are these sounds affirming your personal happiness, or are they serving to block you from ever getting close to anything you dream of having or being in life?

When you first recognized the power of language, you can immediately see an opportunity to change your life. It does not take much for you to notice how negative your language is, and how deeply ingrained in your language is your fears and anxieties about life.

Consider the negative inner chatter that fills your head every single day: "you're too fat, too slow, too stupid, and too late."

All of us are guilty of a long list of inner criticisms. Unfortunately, all that inner chatter is debilitating in a very real sense. Our negative language takes us down, lowers our frequency, and makes the possible impossible.

It speaks to all your fears and blocks, all the reasons why you hold yourself back, and all the ways that you sabotaged your success. The more you listen to the words you use about yourself and your world, the more you see why you draw so much pain into your life. By this simple clarification on your negative thoughts, you can realize just how powerful simple word and thoughts actually are.

One of the first lessons you need to learn is to change your language, to start introducing "loving language" to your vocabulary. This means that you need to learn to actively listen to yourself and to others. You need to acknowledge the fears, the doubts, the pain, that your negative language represents, and then to actively shift the energy by reframing the words into affirming, loving language.

It is not enough to work on just changing the words; you can affirm yourself into big trouble if you do not pay attention. There is a reason why you are in a negative mode. You are unhappy, afraid, angry, something... something that needs to be attended to before positive affirming language can really help. However, once you acknowledge whatever that something is, once you learn to listen to yourself and notice what it is that you are afraid or resentful of, or angry or anxious about, and then also reframed the words to be more affirming, you will see that you have a very powerful tool for changing your life.

Here are some examples of our negative, unloving, low vibration language, and some ways of reframing these statements or changing the words to bring the vibration up so it attracts more of what you want in life.

LEARNING TO USE THE RIGHT WORDS

There are times when NO is the right answer, and NOT helps define a clear boundary, so there is no reason to try to eradicate these words from your vocabulary. However, there is a real need for us each to notice how often and when we are using these words, and to understand their effect on the subconscious.

The subconscious doesn't register qualifying, descriptive language. So when you say: "I'm not going," the subconscious registers: "I'm going."

Do you ever wonder why you ended up going to that function that you definitely had no intention of going to? The more often you said no, the more you affirmed the likelihood that you would go. That is how our kids wear us down. So, instead of saying "I'm not going," say: "I have something else to do that evening." It is a safer way of saying "no."

The same logic applies to the use of "un" and "dis" words. The subconscious hears the active part of the word and therefore nullifies to a large extent the statement you make.

When you say you are "unhappy," or you "dislike," the inner you registers that you are "happy" and you "like." Instead, try replacing the statement with something specific like, "I feel depressed about..." or "my job is unsatisfying..."

THE MEDIUMSHIP OF SPIRIT

NUMBERS IN LIMBO

In 1992, a paranormal investigator named Helmut Schmidt set up a radioactive decay counter to generate sequences of random numbers, both positive and negative. The numbers were recorded, but not seen by any person. Several months later, these numbers were shown to a group of students who had been asked to use their "mind power" to skew the sequences in favor of positive numbers. Elaborate precautions were taken to prevent cheating.

According to fundamental physical laws, there should have been an equal number of positive and negative numbers. But Schmidt reported that the students saw more positive numbers; the probability of that happening was less than 1 in a 1,000.

Did the students actually influence the outcome of radioactive decay rates recorded months before? Henry Stapp, a theoretical physicist at UC Berkeley, thought so.

Stapp was one of the independent monitors of Schmidt's experiments. Two years later, he published a possible explanation for what had happened. In essence, he suggested that human consciousness had interacted with the numbers, effectively altering the past (when the numbers were recorded).

The idea, which Stapp and others have since expanded upon and promoted, is that human consciousness is an unexplained, nonlinear force of nature. Like subatomic particles in quantum mechanics, the numbers in Schmidt's experiment existed in a sort of limbo in which they were positive, negative and neither until the students saw them. At that point, human consciousness and intent (instructions to think positive) induced the numbers to assume a specific condition or quantum state. Science is now coming around to the idea that thought is reality, thought has power.

The physics of consciousness is controversial, to say the least. And Stapp is first to say much more study and experimentation is necessary, especially by respected scientists in well-regarded scientific journals.

"You'd think people would want to either refute or confirm some of these reports," said Stapp, "but the only people willing to test them are people who already tend to believe them. Most mainstream labs shy away for fear of sullying their reputations, as if they would be dirtying their hands by even imagining some of this is possible."

What do you want from life? If you can think up ten things that you want right away, then most likely you would not be reading this book. However, if you are like most people, you find yourself feeling uncertain, a bit uncomfortable, or even guilty when you ask yourself that question. Why do you think that this is? After all, God wants us to be happy.

We have all been conditioned to overlook our personal wants and needs in favor of the group desires. We sublimate our thoughts, and language, hiding our true selves behind the greater good.

As time passes, most of us lose sight of what we really want, think or feel. We might be able to name the next car, house, book, dress, or computer upgrade that we want, but we won't be able to speak in specific terms about what we want for ourselves in life. Most of us simply can not find the words to express our deepest needs and desires.

Many relationships break down because partners cannot specify their needs, or are afraid to be blunt about what works and does not work for them. We hold all of these unspoken expectations of each other and of life in general, and then we wonder why we can't get what we want out of life. How do you expect anyone to satisfy your needs if you cannot speak of them? Even God wants to know what you need and want.

This concept of specificity applies to all we say, think and feel. It is only with clear, specific language that we can create change.

For example, when you say "I don't like you," you leave me no room to negotiate or change your opinion. However, if you say "I don't like your taste in clothes," then I have something to work with. I can decide that pleasing you is worth taking a look at the types of clothes I wear, or I can decide that it's not important to please you on this specific issue. What is important is that by being specific about what you don't like, you affirm the possibility of change, without destroying my self-esteem.

A lack of specificity in one's language attracts a lot of static to your communications. General, uncommitted language hides the conflicts, the unresolved issues. These conflicts act like static on the line, making it difficult for folks to hear you clearly.

THE MEDIUMSHIP OF SPIRIT

If words have vibrational frequency and the higher frequencies attract good stuff to you, then it makes sense to opt for using clear specific language, how else can you clearly and specifically direct the flow of energy around you to create exactly what you want?

Magick spells, curses, blessings and invocations are ways of invoking the power of words. All who teach the ceremonial use of language will also teach the need to be exceptionally clear and specific in any incantation or prayer. Otherwise, things can go terribly wrong.

We invoke the real power of language when we are clear and concise in our choice of words. The more specific you are with the words you use, the more clearly focused is the energy. And clear focused energy is at the root of every success.

So, the next time someone asks you what you want, take some time, to think about your answer and then respond with a clear specific statement: "I want a new, better paying job in six months." Or, "I want a lasting, loving relationship this year."

We also need to address the overuse of the word "should." Every time we use the word should, we are reacting to a judgment, of ourselves or others. Usually, these are unhealthy judgments, expectations that are conditioned as opposed to real.

for example: "I should work harder" – speaks to your judgment that you are lazy, are not good enough, and every time you make this statement you are driving yourself down as opposed to up. However, if, every time you hear yourself about to make this statement, you instead say: "I work smart, all my activities are productive," you will find to your amazement that you are indeed working smart and being far more productive than you have ever been

"Should" implies lack, inadequacy and fear. Shoulds reinforce a kind of poverty-consciousness of the soul. They hold us in our "nots" and discourage us from taking positive affirmative action. If you use negative words it tends to cloud your actual intentions. Negative words leads to negative thoughts. These will then cloud and misdirect your manifestation. Rather than saying: "I don't want this to happen." Instead say: "I WANT this to happen." Now the Universe has something positive to work with.

THE MEDIUMSHIP OF SPIRIT

THE ENERGY OF WORDS

The message in all of this is to seek loving language. Love energy is affirming, balancing and honest. When we learn to speak with the integrity of true love, to be specific in our choice of words, and then to choose words that are loving, positive, affirming – even in describing a challenge that we are facing – we discover an amazing power. Suddenly, with age-old problems, solutions appear, the journey to achieving goals, and finding happiness becomes a simpler, smoother path. Invoke the power of loving language in your life and then stand back to enjoy the magic that ensues.

Words have power, and loving words have the power to make life magical. So start today by looking at your words and thoughts, consider how each and every statement that you think and say can be shifted towards the positive and away from the negative. It may turn out to be the most significant change you will ever make in your life.

ENERGY WORDS EXERCISE

Here is a simple exercise to help you start noticing your low frequency language and then to shift it to a more positive affirming vibrational frequency.

You will need a notebook or journal for this exercise. For the next week, take 15 minutes every day to journal the events of the day and then five minutes to list what you want and what you are afraid of.

Beginning on the second day, after you have completed your journal entries for the day, review everything you have written from the beginning of the week. Notice the negative, low-frequency language and take an additional 15 minutes to rewrite any negative statements with energy words, loving language.

By the end of the week, you will probably notice that there are far fewer low frequency words in your journal, and that you are also correcting your spoken language. As well, you will probably also notice that the week has been easier, that things came more easily to you.

THE MEDIUMSHIP OF SPIRIT

It is amazing how just by changing a few words that we speak or think that our lives can be changed as well. Take the time to examine how you speak and think. Take the time to examine how the energy of your thoughts and words has a very real and significant influence on the direction that your life takes.

If you are truly interested in achieving your goals in life...if you are truly interested in being happy and prosperous, think it, and then say it. Do not hesitate, do not think that you are not worthy of happiness. You are worthy. We all are. But in order to find happiness, we must first make it real in our minds and then in our words.

SIX: The Choice

I now was faced with another choice. I could continue on, into the worlds of spirit, or I could go back to the physical. My old life, my old body was gone. That time on Earth had come and gone just as I had planned from the start.

But as for all of us, I could start a new life on Earth right now. I could choose to be reborn in a new body, in a new timeline. I did not even have to go on to the higher astral planes, I could make my choice right here and now...in the in-between...that place that is neither Earth, nor Heaven.

For many, many souls, there is no choice. They come from Earth too stained, too damaged to be able to lift into the higher realities. Their recent life weighs on them like boulders tied around the neck, dragging them back down to seek the smoky, red light of copulating couples. The siren song of the material world draws these souls like moths to the flame.

This is the way it is. It seems to be unfair, but it actually is the natural way that God has provided us with a way to learn and grow as spiritual beings. We learn from our mistakes. We learn from doing it ourselves. No one can tell us what we should, or should not do. It is for each and every one of us to learn on our own.

Eventually, after many, many lives, our souls enter the in-between with less and less weighing us down. Our minds are cleaner, clearer. We have a better control of our thoughts and a realization that life continues on after physical death. At this point we can make the decision whether or not we should return to Earth right away, or wait a while.

Even at this point, the physical still tempts me. It calls me with a promise of new days, new loves, new pleasures and pains. Yes, even pain. For how are we to know pleasure without having tasted delicious pain? But I was also being called upwards to a new task. The choice was made.

THE MEDIUMSHIP OF SPIRIT

SEVEN: The Spirit of Abundance

WE have been taught from the beginning that we should remove ourselves from the desire for money, prosperity and material desires. "The love of money is the root of all evil" we are told. We can see proof of this all around us everyday.

Crime is usually caused by the desire to have something that has been denied us. We are constantly bombarded by the media with images of desire: expensive jewelry, new clothes, a new car, a bigger, better house, and a big screen television with surround sound. We are nothing unless we own all of these things.

So the questions need to be asked: is it wrong to want money? Is it immoral to desire things? The answer is a definitive maybe.

Actually there is nothing wrong with wanting to be comfortable, to be able to afford things. We live in the material world so it is only natural that we should want and have material things. Where we get into trouble is the lust for money, the lust for stuff, the lust for power. This is where crime comes from: the lust for things that cannot be fulfilled. This is where we stain our souls by becoming obsessed with getting what we do not have, by any means possible.

God the Creator wants us to have things. He wants us to be happy. There is nothing wrong with money and enjoying the benefits of having money. That is unless you are hurting others to get or to hold on to your money and possessions.

It is possible to have your desires. The Universe is vibrating in resonance with you, waiting to help you achieve your goals. As well, there are spirits who are ready to help you, spirits of loved ones who have passed on before you. They are eager to help you in anyway that they can. The key is that you have to know what it is that you really want. You have to decide what it is that will make you happy. All you have to do is ask.

When you are aligned with the invincible forces of the Universe, desired goals materialize very quickly. But if you have contradictory desire streams, desires for two opposing things at the same time, it becomes much more difficult for your spirit friends to fulfill your desires.

THE MEDIUMSHIP OF SPIRIT

Whatever you want, whatever you desire to become, the Universe and your spirit guides act to create that for you. This is a desire world. Actions quickly create results here. When does your life transform? When you consistently work toward a goal with dedication. This is true regardless of what your particular goal happens to be. Haven't you ever wanted something intensely? How did it come to you? Did you work hard to create the means to make it happen? Or did it effortlessly flow to you?

For example, you might think that you desire an ideal relationship, but if part of your brain is thinking, "Fool, you don't deserve that. It's never worked for you before. Why should be so lucky?"

These are split desire streams. Fulfilling the desire for an ideal relationship becomes difficult or impossible. If your past was painful, if your childhood environment was abusive, if you had no role models for a proper relationship, then the task of structuring a healthy, evolving relationship seems much more difficult, may perhaps appear impossible. Thus the conflict continues.

It is similar with the desire for health. Everyone has the inherent capability of being perfectly aligned with great health. From excessive abusive habits of thought and body, the native intelligence of the body is overwhelmed.

It is not necessary to actively work to be healthy; it is only necessary to stop undermining the body's natural ability to be healed. Perfect health is our birthright. Disease is a mistake born from sad dreams of failure and fear.

The effect of our thoughts is easily seen in the body. Every thought, every feeling produces biochemical responses throughout the immune system. If you are happy or in love, your body responds by making you healthy, if you are sad or angry, your body responds in kind by making you sick.

If you alternate between joy and sadness, the body responds by making you sometimes healthy and sometimes sick. Life can be very long or very short; this is determined by the quality of your thought much more than the quality of your food, air or water.

THE MEDIUMSHIP OF SPIRIT

If you have a desire for enlightenment, the same principles of the Universe are at work. Some say they wish to be enlightened but don't really believe it is possible. Others attempt for a while to move ahead but are not willing to break the attachments to beliefs that cripple their expansion into the Infinite One. Others desire enlightenment for the wrong reasons, to control others, or to gain wealth or power. All such will never succeed. God the Creator is perfectly willing to outwait such lustful material desires.

Even if it takes all of eternity, the Universe will patiently wait for a soul to desire reunification with Creation. It is not possible to serve two masters.

When one realizes that there is a reason for human existence and aligns with that purpose, life becomes supremely simple. Until that day, life is divided between the world and the spirit. And God patiently waits, and waits for us to realize our foolish ways.

Human consciousness is sufficiently subtle to influence the natural laws that uphold the progression of the Universe. Human desire stirs the waters of the cosmic sea; they rise in waves to fulfill our every impulse of thought.

This is not commonly observed because desires are often opposed, the Universe tries to fulfill them but cannot because opposite things are desired, or the desires are so numerous that our spirit guides do not have sufficient time to fulfill them. On the other hand, when we learn to entertain one desire at a time, the time required to fulfill the desire shrinks, and the more consistently one desire is entertained without introducing opposing thoughts, the more quickly it can be fulfilled.

DON'T BE AFRAID OF CHANGE

To be able to focus your mind to one desire at a time, we have to be able to except change. Change is challenging whether it is conscious or unexpected. Viewing adversity as change, not loss or failure, is part of empowered and positive thinking. Humans develop resiliency through change, both physiologically, and emotionally. It is necessary for all life forms to evolve. Change comes though many vehicles — some hit us hard, others are rather sneaky. But despite the challenges change brings, we know it is our natural state — the world grows and we grow with it fueled by our emotions. We are already designed to cry, express sorrow, frustration, anger, and resentment and most of us choose to explore these feelings. But we are also designed to have hope, recover, be stronger, and inspire others as a result of change. You are never alone because emotion gives us plenty in common, as a society.

What makes one person triumphantly survive loss and turn it into positive energy, while another in similar circumstances resign? It has to do with our underlying assumptions on change.

Certainly, our culture has become more comfortable with making choices that have predictable outcomes. A current cultural disease we suffer from is predictability, reflected in our inability to accept change at a deeply personal level. It applies across the board to choices we make with our finances, careers, or our relationships.

Science, especially when applied to health issues, has given us a false security blanket when it comes to certainty. After all, it seems we've been able to control nature. We like to think we've cornered the market on predictability and good planning, when the truth is we live in a time where prediction is more intuition and common sense than science.

To embrace change, we need to release the umbilical cord we think we have to outcomes of certainty. In other words, stepping off of the plateau requires a huge amount of trust. Your fall will be broken somewhere at the right time.

Believing that is what allows us to cope. It is the first step, unsupported by any scientific doctrine. And it's a big one. No matter what science pronounces, whether it is in the form of a diagnosis or the state of the environment, there is no sure thing. Science has already given us permission to accept truth with a margin of error in just about anything. There is always the possibility something may exist or not exist, despite what patterns indicate.

It is a useless endeavor to let science hold you back from moving forward. Whether it is health, or other issues surrounding job loss, divorce, or death, you will successfully navigate through change and elevate the quality of your life by knowing anyone can beat the odds.

THE MEDIUMSHIP OF SPIRIT

Almost everyone you know has a story of beating the odds. Let's pay attention to the real evidence instead of looking for ways to prove that we cannot make it or the odds are just too great. Adopting a new attitude on adversity requires big picture thinking on the subject of change.

View life, and spiritual development for that matter, as an upward spiral where you experience some of the same lessons over and over again. When you do this, you create new possibilities, new realities for yourself.

Is it because we just aren't getting what the lesson is telling us? Perhaps, but that is not the only reason. We have deliberately put those circumstances in our chart in frequent doses to allow ourselves an opportunity to see how we've been progressing on the upward part of that growth spiral.

Adversity is an inescapable performance indicator, a frequent reminder of our upcoming 360-degree review in how we handle the bumps. We are meant to be stronger, more insightful each time we get knocked down.

EXPECTING A MIRACLE

Have you ever had an overwhelming problem or issue? Was there some circumstance in your life that seemed beyond your ability to handle it? Have you ever called out to God, your higher self, your spirit guides?

Have you cried out to God the Creator for help with some crisis in your life? Did you get help? When we get the help and assistance, we assume all is well in the heavens. We think, "Wow! Miracles really do happen!"

However, when we don't get the answer or the help, we often conclude that there is no God. We seem to have mixed up our traditional beliefs stating that we have to jump through hoops and beg for our spirit guides to favor us, and the new age concepts that we can simply visualize anything we want into manifesting.

Positive visualization and faith are intertwined. You really cannot have one without the other. You cannot empower your visualizations without faith. Faith is not sitting around doing nothing while demanding miracles from the spirits to come and save you. If you have made choices that have put you into a bad place, don't yell at the spirits to come and help you out. Don't just sit there doing nothing while expecting the heavens to fix it all for you. It is not their job. It's your job.

Faith is trusting that if you work hard at finding solutions to your problems while following the Golden Rule, then things will turn out for the best. It is believing that your spirit guides will help you find or cultivate the solutions you need. The Golden Rule, karma, what comes around goes around, cause and effect, exists. If you make bad choices, bad things will happen. If you hurt people, people will hurt you. If you're living a negative lifestyle, then cry out for the gods to come save you from your misery, you're not likely to get any help. It's your life, your problems. Learn, grow, heal, and move forward.

You can tell your spirit guide you are sorry for your part in creating the problem and that you're ready to change it. Then prove it, by changing it. God the Creator will show itself somewhere along the way. Have faith and keep working at it.

Let us assume it is one of those times in life where you were happily going along doing your good deeds, having a positive attitude, and some nightmare blew up in your face anyway. What is your immediate response when that happens?

Do you claim there is no God and that all of your positive thoughts and deeds were of no use Do you lose faith that your God will guide you through the event? Or, do you hold strong to your God and to your positive beliefs? Do you roll up your sleeves and get to work on finding solutions? Do you even find ways to continue seeing the beauty in life while overcoming the adversity?

Negative people who do not have much faith in themselves, in life, their spirit guides, or in God, tend to use life's adversities as proof that they are correct for being so pessimistic. On the other hand, people who are upbeat and positive, having faith in themselves and in life, tend to use adversities to collect evidence that everything really does turn out for the best in the long run. Whether we believe in God or not doesn't affect whether or not there is some form of God.

THE MEDIUMSHIP OF SPIRIT

When we have faith that things will get better, they usually do. When we believe things will not get better, they probably won't.

Do miracles happen? Absolutely. They happen to all kinds of people all the time. They happen regardless of religion, gender or financial position. By definition, they have a magical unexplainable mystery element that's integral to how it came to be. Whatever the forces are that cause such things to happen, it is truly awe inspiring.

Can you force miracles to happen by demanding them or by blackmailing your spirit friends with the underlying belief system that if your miracle is not delivered then you are going to turn your back on your God? Definitely not. You can coax them by recognizing them when they happen no matter how little they might be and by being thankful to whatever force you attribute them to: "Thank you for your divine intervention, whoever you are."

This choice is so much easier to make than is commonly believed. There is no difficulty in being enlightened; there is no problem that is so large the Infinite cannot heal it or solve it; there is nothing that can stand in the way of the dawn of perfection other than refusing to make the one choice that matters. When any human sees this choice clearly, it becomes absurdly easy to make it. Then the human ceases to be human and becomes divine.

There is nothing that cannot be accomplished by one-pointed faith; there is nothing we will not do in order to heal the Earth. Stay tuned and watch. Miracles will happen. You will be amazed.

TALKING TO YOUR GUIDES

We all have non-physical beings ready, willing and able to help us at any time. There are angels, spiritual beings who have never lived a physical life, who want to help you to be happier, healthier, more at peace, and totally enjoying your life.

Your angels know what your mission in life is. They know what your true talents are, and your angels also know that you can have more joy and fun out of life while minimizing conflict and despair.

THE MEDIUMSHIP OF SPIRIT

While we can grow from conflict, we can also grow from having peace. That is the angels' mission, to build world peace, one person at a time. Whatever brings you peace, the angels are very happy to help you find it.

There are your spirit guides – these are your loved ones and ancestors who have passed on, and you have at least one with you most of the time. Usually, they are relatives and friends who you knew before they passed. Occasionally, they are relatives who passed before you were born.

In addition, there are Ascended Masters. These are great teachers and healers who once walked upon the Earth. They have raised their consciousness to a level that has allowed them to bypass the merry-go-round of reincarnation. They have ascended to the higher realms of the astral worlds. They too can help you.

You have help available to you at anytime. They can help you more if you will remember a few things. First, you've got to ask for their help and you can ask in a number of different ways.

You can say the request aloud or you can think it, as they do hear your thoughts. Or you can write the request down on a piece of paper or even on your computer. You can even sing or shout it loud.

You can ask affirmatively: "Thank you for helping me." Or as a prayer of supplication: "Please help me." You can command it: "Help me now." It does not matter how you ask, what matters is that you ask for help.

Many people who think that Heaven is ignoring them are not asking for help. Secondly, do not tell the spirits to help you. The Divine wisdom knows how to help you in a way that will best suit your situation. Just ask for help and then let them get to work.

After that you will receive help in one of several ways – most commonly, you will get Divine guidance. This means repetitive thoughts, feelings, words, coincidence, or visions that direct you to take action or, the angels will directly intervene.

You ask for a new job, and the phone rings with an old friend offering you a job, for example. Sometimes, the angels will appear in human form temporarily to help you. The angel gives you a message that helps you, or performs some life-saving assistance.

You can ask for help with big or little things, it does not matter, because "matter" doesn't matter to the spirit world. All that matters is love. So ask for anything that you sincerely believe will bring you or your loved ones happiness.

You can ask for as many favors as you need, like during the day you can ask for protection, to receive healings, or for a better relationship, or more abundance. All requests are heard and answered. You just have to accept that it is OK to ask for help.

Remember, it is important to put your thoughts only in the direction of your desires. Never allow yourself to think about your fears. Your thoughts are reality. Do not let your thoughts become negative.

This choice is easier to make than is commonly believed. There is no difficulty in being enlightened; there is no problem that is so large the Infinite cannot heal it or solve it; there is nothing that can stand in the way of the dawn of perfection other than refusing to make the right choice.

A PROSPERITY PRAYER

You can recite this prayer once a day when you are seeking a particular desire or goal. After reciting this prayer, ask your spirit guides, guardian angel, or Ascended Master for help with whatever you seek.

You can also recite this prayer everyday simply to acknowledge your devotion to God the Creator and to remind yourself that you and God are the real masters of your reality.

I live in an abundant Universe - I always have everything I need. I create money and abundance through joy, aliveness, and self-love. My energy is focused and directed toward my goals. I focus on what I love and thus draw it to me. My thoughts are loving and positive. I choose the path of most light. I honor myself in everything I do. I am in integrity in all that I do. My beliefs create my reality – I believe in my unlimited prosperity.

Money flows into my life – I am prosperous. I speak of success and prosperity - My words uplift and inspire others. I live in an abundant world – All is perfect in my universe. I surrender to my higher good. As I do what I love, abundance flows freely to me. I am linked with the unlimited abundance of the Universe.

Miracles are love in action. I have a unique, special contribution to make. Everything I do adds beauty, harmony, order and light to the Universe. I am in charge of my destiny – I am the builder of my life. The Universe is safe, abundant and friendly.

I follow my heart. I commit to my path – I choose aliveness and growth. I invite and allow good to come into my life. I flow like a river and so does my prosperity. I bring love & a positive attitude to everything I do. All the money I spend enriches society and comes back to me multiplied. Everything I give to others is a gift to me – As I give, so do I receive.

Every gift I give others honors and acknowledges their worth. All my money is ever awaiting my command to create good in my life. I give generously to myself. I serve others to the best of my ability in all I say and do. I am always being guided to the Higher Solution. I choose to live an abundant life.

EIGHT: To Guide Others

THERE are many phases of reality. Each exists on its own vibrational level. The material world exists in a lower vibrational state than the worlds of spirit. The worlds of spirit, or the astral worlds, exist in increasingly higher levels of vibration.

When we first leave our physical body, our soul tends to be attracted to the vibrational level that best suits it at that very moment. For those who lived their lives with no thought of themselves or others, the only choice is to be reborn to pay off the karmic debt and learn how to take the soul out of the cosmic merry-go-round of birth-death-and rebirth.

I had now made the decision to remove myself from the wheel of life and death. This does not mean that I won't choose to return to Earth later on, but now I had a different mission that needed to be handled from the world of spirit.

Once again my mind was free from the handicaps of the physical world. It is much like awakening from a dream and everything becomes crystal clear. The Universe is mental. We exist in the mind of the All. That part of us which is deity makes up the world and everything in it.

We exist in all planes, astral as well as physical. Or rather planes independent of the physical. As above, so below; as below, so above.

Just as my Ascended Masters assisted me during my life, it was now my mission to assist others on the Earth plane. The energy of reality now flows through me, unhampered by the filters of the physical. Knowledge is energy and cannot be destroyed. Time is an illusion and has no meaning. There are an infinite number of pasts and an infinite number of futures. All is now.

The message, however, is not so easily transferred from here to there. For those who are willing to listen, to take the time to master their thoughts and quiet the mind, the message becomes clear. It is all so easy.

NINE: So You Want to Live Forever

THE desire to live is hardwired into our genes. We all have an innate sense within us that it is possible for us to live much longer than we currently do.

Of course we are all immortal. Our souls are a part of Creation, and Creation is forever; but what about our physical bodies? Is it possible for us to live longer, much longer than the current extreme of a little more than 100 years? The answer is an unequivocal YES. We were created to live a long and fruitful life. Our bodies are meant to be self-repairing and are perfectly capable of living for hundreds of years.

The Bible lists many people who lived for hundreds of years. In fact, in the book of Genesis the Elohim refer to two trees in the Garden of Eden, the Tree of Knowledge and the Tree of Life. Once Adam and Eve had eaten from the Tree of Knowledge, the Elohim had no choice but to chase them out of Eden for fear that they would eat of the Tree of Life and become immortal. Other ancient texts also state that in the far past people lived much longer than they do today.

So we know that it is possible. But the way we live today makes extreme longevity almost impossible. We often depend on drugs that keep us "virtually" alive. A typical modern human would not be able to survive the environmental conditions to which ancient humans have adapted over many years of evolution.

The truth is that behind the facade of all the cosmetics and expensive outfits, there lies a biologically dysfunctional modern human who may likely be considered an evolutionary setback by future anthropologists. Eating, eliminating and reproducing are the most basic biological functions of any living species. The inability to perform these biological functions leaves many people living virtually, in bodies that are gradually shifting from their original self-sustaining nature toward an increasing dependency on chemicals and calories.

In spite of the gradual degradation of the modern human body, deep inside each of us there is a primal survival mechanism that can direct us on how to follow our biological destiny and thereby reach both physical and mental superiority.

THE MEDIUMSHIP OF SPIRIT

There is no manmade machine that can do what your body can do, that is, to recreate itself. The human body, like any other life form, is preprogrammed to continuously recreate itself. It is this regenerating mechanism that literally carries within each of us the secret to immortality.

Deep within each of us is a primal switch that once turned on starts a regenerative mechanism to recycle old tissue, build new brain cells, improve the muscle to fat ratio, enhance immunity, ignite energy and keep us vigorous. The failure to understand that fact and instead follow wrong feeding cycles keeps this regenerative switch shut off. Poor diet may indeed be the culprit for most health problems including chronic diseases, advanced aging, weight gain, obesity, sexual dysfunction, depression and mental impairments.

The right kinds of foods are essential for an increased lifespan. Stay away from processed foods. I know that they are easy and convenient, but they are also full of salt, sugar, fats, and chemicals that do nothing for your health, and in fact add to your body's slow deterioration. Eat fresh fruits, vegetables, grains, beans and fish. Meat is OK on a limited basis, say once or twice a week. Consuming vegetables and fruits mostly of green, yellow, orange and red color will supply your body with the essential vitamins, minerals, fiber and antioxidants.

Eating mushrooms, whole grains, legumes, herbs and spices will give the body essential fiber and polysaccharides as well as immuno-supportive compounds that help support all basic metabolic functions.

Eating nuts and seeds and consuming essential oils that contain omega-3 and omega-6 EFAs should supply the essential fatty acids required for all metabolic functions. Eating fresh yogurt everyday is especially good as this supplies the body with probiotics.

Nevertheless, life is not always about getting by on the minimum. Those who wish to excel and trigger overall growth and rejuvenation should view nutritional support as more than just covering the basics or simply getting enough calories. It is important to realize that diet and lifestyle should always come first. There are no nutritional supplements that can compensate for poor eating habits and a lack of exercise. Nutrition should never be regarded as fuel per se. When trained properly, the body can be more efficient in turning fat storage into energy than in turning a ham sandwich into energy.

Attention leads to immortality. Carelessness leads to death. Those who pay attention will not die, while the careless are as good as dead already. Immortality is a state, not eternal embodiment–in this or some other realm–and consequently identified with "I am this, I am that." To transcend both birth and death is immortality, is eternity.

Since it leads to immortality, attention is definitely more than simple awareness or even insight. It is "earnestness in doing good," in pursuing the sole good: liberation. Naturally, a great deal more than attention is needed, but without its dynamic all the other requisites are worthless, like machines without the energy to run them.

Death is not divestment of a body, but immersion in the relative world of spirit and its bonds. It, too, is a state, even though external conditions necessarily follow and mirror its presence.

"Life" in any relative condition is really death, because it shrouds the truth of our essential being. "Carelessness" is the opposite of attention, and is the way we all lead our lives, physical and psychological. If that were not so, none of us would be here. We neither see nor deal with anything in a realistic manner. Frankly, we are profoundly delusional, and our only hope is the correct pursuit of ultimate reality–which is ultimate freedom. Consequently we pray: "Lead me from death to immortality."

We have to love our lives in order for our lives to be worth living. We need to love ourselves and those around us. A happy life, a full life, with friends and family is one of the main keys to a long and fruitful life.

Except that fact that you have the ability to live forever; treat your body and soul with respect and love. Take a walk and look at the world around you. Listen to the sounds of life, breath in the smells of Creation. Live each and every day with no thought of yesterday or tomorrow.

Sleep well, eat well, love well, and live well.

Become one with Creation and allow yourself to be immortal.

TEN: Thoughts Made Real

THERE belongs to every human being a higher self and a lower self—a self or mind of the spirit which has been growing for ages, and a self of the body, which is but a thing of yesterday. The higher self is full of prompting idea, suggestion and aspiration. This it receives of the Supreme Power. All this the lower or animal self regards as wild and visionary.

The higher self argues possibilities and power for us greater than men and women now possess and enjoy. The lower self says we can only live and exist as men and women have lived and existed before us. The higher self craves freedom from the cumbrousness, the limitations, the pains and disabilities of the body. The lower self says that we are born to them, born to ill, born to suffer, and must suffer as have so many before us.

The higher self wants a standard for right and wrong of its own. The lower self says we must accept a standard made for us by others—by general and long-held opinion, belief and prejudice. "To thine own self be true" is an oft-uttered adage. But to which self? The higher or lower? You have in a sense two minds—the mind of the body and the mind of the spirit. Spirit is a force and a mystery. All we know or may ever know of it is that it exists, and is ever working and producing all results in physical things seen of physical sense and many more not so seen.

What is seen, of any object, a tree, an animal, a stone, a man is only a part of that tree, animal, stone, or man. There is a force which for a time binds such objects together in the form you see them. That force is always acting on them to greater or lesser degree. It builds up the flower to its fullest maturity. Its cessation to act on the flower or tree causes what we call decay. It is constantly changing the shape of all forms of what are called organized matter.

An animal, a plant, a human being are not in physical shape this month or this year what they will be next month or next year. This ever-acting, ever-varying force, which lies behind and, in a sense, creates all forms of matter we call Spirit. To see, reason and judge of life and things in the knowledge of this force makes what is termed the "Spiritual Mind." We have through knowledge the wonderful power of using or directing this force, when we recognize it, and know that it exists so as to bring us health, happiness and eternal peace of mind. Composed as we are of this force, we are ever attracting more of it to us and making it a part of our being. With more of this force must come more and more knowledge.

At first in our physical existences we allow it to work blindly. Then we are in the ignorance of that condition known as the material mind. But as mind through its growth or increase of this power becomes more and more awakened, it asks: "Why comes so much of pain, grief and disappointment in the physical life?" "Why do we seem born to suffer and decay" That question is the first awakening cry of the spiritual mind, and an earnest question or demand for knowledge must in time be answered.

The material mind is a part of yourself, which has been appropriated by the body and educated by the body. It is as if you taught a child that the wheels of a steamboat made the boat move, and said nothing of the steam, which gives the real power.

Bred in such ignorance, the child, should the wheels stop moving, would look no farther for the cause of their stoppage than to try to find where to repair them, very much as now so many depend entirely on repair of the physical body to ensure its healthy, vigorous movement, never dreaming that the imperfection lies in the real motive power–the mind. The mind of the body or material mind sees, thinks and judges entirely from the material or physical standpoint. It sees in your own body all there is of you.

The spiritual mind sees the body as an instrument for the mind or real self to use in dealing with material things. The material mind sees in the death of the body an end of all there is of you. The spiritual mind sees in the death of the body only the falling off from the spirit of a worn-out instrument. It knows that you exist as before only invisible to the physical eye.

The material mind sees your physical strength as coming entirely from your muscles and sinews, and not from source without your body. It sees in such persuasive power, as you may have with tongue or pen, the only force you possess for dealing with people to accomplish results. The spiritual mind will know in time that your thought influences people for or against your interests, though their bodies are thousands of miles distant.

THE MEDIUMSHIP OF SPIRIT

The material mind does not regard its thought as an actual element as real as air or water. The spiritual mind knows that every one of its thousand daily secret thoughts are real things acting on the minds of the persons they are sent to.

The spiritual mind knows that matter or the material is only an expression of spirit or force; that such matter is ever changing in accordance with the spirit that makes or externalizes itself in the form we call matter, and therefore, if the thought of health, strength and recuperation is constantly held to in the mind, such thought of health, strength and rejuvenation will express itself in the body, making maturity never ceasing, vigor never ending, and the keenness of every physical sense ever increasing.

The material mind thinks matter, or that which is known by our physical senses, to be the largest part of what exists. The spiritual mind regards matter as the coarser or cruder expression of spirit and the smallest part of what really exists. The material mind is made sad at the contemplation of decay. The spiritual mind attaches little importance to decay, knowing in such decay that spirit or the moving force in all things is simply taking the dead body or the rotten tree to pieces, and that it will build them up again as before temporarily into some other new physical form of life and beauty.

The mind of the body thinks that its physical senses of seeing, hearing and feeling constitute all the senses you possess. The higher mind or mind of the spirit knows that it possesses other senses akin to those of physical sight and hearing, but more powerful and far reaching. The mind of the body has been variously termed "the material mind," the "mortal mind" and the "carnal mind." All these refer to the same mind, or, in other words to that part of your real sell which has been educated in error by the body.

If you had been born and bred entirely among people who believed that the earth was a flat surface and did not revolve around the sun, you would in the earlier years of your physical growth believe as they did. Exactly in such fashion do you in your earlier years absorb the thought and belief of those nearest you, who think that the body is all there is of them, and judge of everything by its physical interpretation to them. This makes your material mind.

THE MEDIUMSHIP OF SPIRIT

The material mind seeing, what seems to it, depth, dissolution and decay in all human organization, and ignorant of the fact that the real self or intelligence has in such seeming death only cast off a worn-out envelope, thinks that decay and death is the ultimate of all humanity. For such reason it cannot avoid a gloom or sadness coming of such error, which now pervades so much of human life at present.

One result or reaction from such gloom born of hopelessness is a reckless spirit for getting every possible gratification and pleasure, regardless of right and justice so long as the present body lasts. This is a great mistake. All pleasure so gained cannot be lasting. It brings besides a hundredfold more misery and disappointment. The spiritual mind teaches that pleasure is the great aim of existence. But it points out ways and means for gaining lasting happiness other than those coming of the teaching of the material mind. The spiritual mind, or mind opened to higher and newer forces of life, teaches that there is a law regulating the exercise of every physical sense.

When we learn and follow this law, our gratifications and possessions do not prove sources of greater pain than happiness, as they do to so many. By the spiritual mind is meant a clearer mental sight of things and forces existing both in us and the Universe, and of which the race for the most part has been in total ignorance.

We have now but a glimpse of these forces, those of some being relatively a little clearer than those of others. But enough has been shown to convince a few that the real and existing causes for humanity's sickness, sorrow and disappointment have not in the past been seen at all. In other words, the race has been as children, fancying that the miller inside was turning the arms of the windmill, because some person had so told them. So taught, they would remain in total ignorance that the wind was the motive power.

This illustration is not at all an overdrawn picture of the existing ignorance which rejects the idea that thought is an element all about us as plentiful as air, and that as blindly directed by individuals and masses of individuals in the domain of material mind or ignorance, it is turning the windmill's arms, sometimes in one direction, sometimes in another; sometimes with good and sometimes with evil results.

THE MEDIUMSHIP OF SPIRIT

A suit of clothes is not the body that wears such suit. Yet the material mind reasons very much in this way. It knows of no such thing as clothing for the spirit, for it does not know that body and spirit are two distinct things. It reasons that the suit of clothing (the body) is all t here is of the man or woman. When that man or woman tumbles to pieces through weakness, it sees only the suit of clothes so going to pieces, and all its efforts to make that man or woman stronger are put on the suit instead of making effort to reinforce the power within which has made the suit.

There are probably no two individuals precisely alike as regards the relative condition or action on them of their material and spiritual minds. With some the spiritual seems not at all awakened. With others it has begun to stretch and rub its eyes as a person does on physical awakening, when everything still appears vague and indistinct. Others are more fully awakened. They feel to greater or lesser extent that there are forces belonging to them before unthought of. It is with such that the struggle for mastery between the material and spiritual mind is likely to be most severe, and such struggle for a time is likely to be accompanied by physical disturbance, pain or lack of ease.

The material mind is, until won over and convinced of the truths, constantly received by the spiritual mind at war and in opposition to it. The ignorant part of yourself dislikes very much to give up its long accustomed habits of thinking. Its costs a struggle in any case at first to own that we have been mistaken and give up views long held to.

The material mind wants to more on in a rut of life and idea, as it always has done, and as thousands are now doing. It dislikes change more and more as the crust of the old thought held from year to year grows more thickly over it. It wants to live on and on in the house it has inhabited for years; dress in the fashion of the past; go to business and return year in and year out at precisely the same hour.

It rejects and despises after a certain age the idea of learning any new accomplishments, such as painting or music, whose greatest use is to divert the mind, rest it, and enable you to live in other departments of being, all this being apart from the pleasure also given you as the mind or spirit teaches the body more and more skill and expertness in the art you pursue.

THE MEDIUMSHIP OF SPIRIT

The material mind sees as the principal use of any art only a means to bring money, and not in such art a means for giving variety to life, dispelling weariness, resting that portion of the mind devoted to other business, improving health and increasing vigor of mind and body. It holds to the idea of being "too old to learn."

This is the condition of so many persons who have arrived at or are past "middle age." They want to "settle down." They accept as inevitable the idea of "growing old." Their material mind tells them that their bodies must gradually weaken, shrink from the fullness and proportion of youth, decay and finally die.

Material minds say this always has been, and therefore always must be. They accept the idea wholly. They say quite unconsciously, "It must be." To say a thing must be, is the very power that makes it. The material mind then sees the body ever as gradually decaying, even though it dislikes the picture, and puts it out of sight as much as possible. But the idea will recur from time to time as suggested by the death of their contemporaries, and as it does they think "must," and that state of mind indicated by the word "must" will inevitably bring material results in decay.

The spiritual or more enlightened mind says: "If you would help to drive away sickness, turn your thought as much as you can on health, strength and vigor, and on strong, healthy, vigorous material things, such as moving clouds, fresh breezes, the cascade, the ocean surge; on woodland scenes and growing healthy trees; on birds full of life and motion; for in so doing you turn on yourself a real current or this healthy life-giving thought, which is suggested and brought you by the thought of such vigorous, strong material objects. And above all, try to rely and trust that Supreme Power which formed all these things and far more and which is the endless and inexhaustible part of your higher self or spiritual mind, and as your faith increases in this Power, so will your own power ever increase.

"Nonsense!" says the ultra material mind." If my body is sick, I must have something done to cure that body with things I can see and feel, and that is the only thing to be done. As for thinking, it makes no difference what I think, sick or well."

At present in such a case a mind whose sense of these truths new to it, has just commenced to be awakened, will, in many cases, allow itself to be for a time overpowered and ridiculed out of such an idea by its own material mind or uneducated part of itself; and in this it is very likely to be assisted by other material minds, who have not woke up at all to these truths, and who are temporarily all the stronger through the positiveness of ignorance.

These are as people who cannot see as far ahead as one may with a telescope, and who may be perfectly honest in their disbelief regarding what the person with the telescope does see. Though such people do not speak a word or argue against the belief of the partly awakened mind, still their thought acts on such a mind as a bar or blind to these glimpses of the truth. But when the spiritual mind has once commenced to awaken, nothing can stop its further waking, though the material may for a time retard it.

"Your real self may not at times be where your body is" says the spiritual mind. It is where your mind is—in the store, the office, the workshop, or with some person to whom you are strongly attached, and all of these may be in towns or cities far from the one your body resides in. Your real self moves with inconceivable rapidity as your thought moves.

"'Nonsense" says your material mind; "I myself am wherever my body is, and nowhere else."

Many a thought or idea that you reject as visionary, or as a whim or fancy, comes of the prompting of your spiritual mind. It is your material mind that rejects it. No such idea comes but that there is a truth in it. But that truth we may not be able to carry out to a relative perfection immediately.

Two hundred years ago some mind may have seen the use of steam as a motive power. But that motive power could not then have been carried out as it is today. A certain previous growth was necessary—a growth and improvement in the manufacture of iron, in the construction of roads, and in the needs of the people. But the idea was a truth.

Held to by various minds, it has brought steam as a motive power to its present relative perfection. It has struggled against and overcome every argument and obstacle placed in its way by dull, material, plodding minds. When you entertain any idea and say to yourself in substance: "Well, such a thing may be, though I cannot now see it" you remove a great barrier to the carrying out and realization by yourself of the new and strange possibilities in store for you.

The spiritual mind today sees belonging to itself a power for accomplishing any and all results in the physical world, greater than the masses dream of. It sees that as regards life's possibilities we are still in dense ignorance. It sees however, a few things—namely, perfect health, freedom from decay, weakness and death of the body, power of transit, travel and observation independent of the body, and methods for obtaining all needful and desirable material things through the action and working of silent mind or thought, either singly or in co-operation with others.

The condition of mind to be desired is the entire dominancy of the spiritual mind. But this does not imply dominancy or control in any sense of tyrannical mastership of the material mind by the spiritual mind. It does imply that the material mind will be swept away so far as its stubborn resistance and opposition to the promptings of the spiritual are concerned.

It implies that the body will become the willing servant, or rather assistant of the spirit. It implies that the material mind will not endeavour to act itself up as the superior when it is only the inferior. It implies that state when the body will gladly lend its co-operation to all the desires of the spiritual mind. Then all power can be given your spirit. Then no force need be expended in resisting the hostility of the material mind. Then all such force will be used to further our undertakings, to bring us material goods, to raise us higher and higher into realms of power, peace and happiness, to accomplish what now would be called miracles. Neither the material mind nor the material body is to be won over and merged into the spiritual by any course of severe self censure or self denial, nor self punishment in expiation for sins committed, nor asceticism. That will only make you the more harsh, severe, bigoted and merciless, both to yourself and others.

It is out of this perversion of the truth that have arisen such terms as "crucifying the body" and "subjugating the lower or animal mind." It is from this perversion that have come orders and associations of men and women who, going to another extreme, seek holiness in self denial and penance.

THE MEDIUMSHIP OF SPIRIT

"Holiness" implies wholeness, or whole action of the spirit on t he body, or perfect control by your spirit over a body, through knowledge and faith in our capacity to draw ever more and more from the Supreme Power. When you get out of patience with yourself, through the aggressiveness of the material mind, through your frequent slips and falls into your besetting sins through period s of petulance or ill temper, or excess in any direction, you do no good, and only ill in calling or thinking for yourself hard names.

You should not call yourself "a vile sinner" anymore than you would call any other person a "vile sinner," If you do, you put out in thought the "vile sinner" and make it temporarily a reality. If in your mental vision you teach yourself that you are "utterly depraved" and a "vile sinner," you are unconsciously making that your ideal, and you will unconsciously grow up to it until the pain and evil coming of such unhealthy growth either makes you turn back or destroys your body, For out of this state of mind, which in the past has been much inculcated, comes harshness, bigotry, lack of charity for others, hard, stern and gloomy and unhealthy views of life, and these mental conditions will surely bring physical disease.

When the material mind is put away, or, in other words, then we become convinced of the existence of these spiritual forces, both in ourselves, and outside of ourselves, and when we learn to use them rightly (for we are now and always have been using them in some way), then to use the words of Paul: "Faith is swallowed up in victory," and the sting and fear of death is removed.

Life becomes then one glorious advance forward from the pleasure of today to the greater pleasure of tomorrow, and the phrase "to live" means only to enjoy.

ELEVEN - Thought Energy

WE need to be careful of what we think and talk. Because thought, for all intents and purposes is energy. Your thought energies, or currents, are as real as those of air and water. Of what we think and talk we attract to us a like current of thought. This acts on mind or body for good or ill. If thought was visible to the physical eye we should see its cur rents flowing to and from people.

We should see that persons similar in temperament, character and motive are in the same literal current of thought. We should see that the person in a despondent and angry mood was in the same current with others despondent or angry, and that each one in such moods serves as an additional battery or generator of such thought and is strengthening that particular current.

We should see these forces working in similar manner and connecting the hopeful, courageous and cheerful, with all others hopeful, courageous and cheerful. When you are in low spirits or "blue" you have acting on you the thought current coming from all others in low spirits. You are in oneness with the despondent order of thought. The mind is then sick. It can be cured, but a permanent cure cannot always come immediately when one has long been in the habit of opening the mind to this current of thought.

In attracting to us the current of any kind of evil, we become for a time one with evil. In the thought current of the Supreme Power for good we may become more and more as one with that power, or in Biblical phrase "One with God." That is the desirable thought current for us to attract. If a group of people talk of any form of disease or suffering, of death-bed scenes and dying agonies, if they cultivate this morbid taste for the unhealthy and ghastly, and it forms their staple topics of conversation, they bring in themselves a like current of thought full of images of sickness, suffering and things revolting to a healthy mind.

This current will act on them, and eventually bring them disease and suffering in some form. If we are talking much of sick people or are much among them and thinking of them, be our motive what it may, we shall draw on ourselves a current of sickly thought, and its ill results will in time materialize itself in our bodies. We have far more to do to save ourselves than is now realized. When men talk business together they attract a business current of idea and suggestion. The better they agree the more of this thought current do they attract and the more do they receive of idea and suggestion for improving and extending their business.

In this way does the conference or discussion among the leading members of the company or corporation create the force that carries their business ahead. Travel in first-class style, put up at first-class hotels and dress in apparel "as costly as your purse can buy," without running into the extreme of foppishness.

In these things you find aids to place you in a current of relative power and success. If your purse does not now warrant such expenditure, or you think it does not, you can commence so living in mind. This will make you take the first steps in this direction. Successful people in the domain of finance unconsciously live up to this law. Desire for show influences some to this course. But there is another force and factor which so impels them. That is a wisdom of which their material minds are scarcely conscious. It is the wisdom of the spirit telling them to get in the thought current of the successful, and by such current be borne to success. It is not a rounded-out success, but good is far as it goes. If our minds are, from what is falsely called economy, ever set on the cheap–cheap lodgings, cheap food and cheap fares, we get in the thought current of the cheap, the slavish and the fearful.

Our views of life and our plans will be influenced and warped by it. It paralyzes that courage and enterprise implied in the old adage "Nothing ventured nothing gained." Absorbed in this current and having it ever acting on you, it is felt immediately when you come into the presence of the successful an d causes them to avoid you. They feel in you the absence of that element which brings them their relative success. It acts as a barrier, preventing the flow to you of their sympathy.

Sympathy is a most important factor in business. Despite opposition and competition, a certain thought current of sympathy binds the most successful together. The mania for cheapness lies in the thought current of fear and failure. The thought current of fear and failure, and the thought current of dash, courage and success will not mingle nor bring together the individuals who are in these respective streams of thought. They antagonize, and between the two classes of mind is built a barrier more impenetrable than walls of stone.

Live altogether in any one idea, any one "reform" and you get into the thought current of all other minds who are carrying that idea to extremes. There is no "reform" but what can be pushed too far. The harm of such extreme falls on the person who so pushes it. It warps mind, judgment and reason all on one side. It makes fanatics, bigots, cranks and lunatics, whether the idea involves an art or study, a science, a "reform" or a "movement." It connects the extremists of all people in such order and current of mind, no matter what their specialties may be. Such people often end in becoming furious haters of all who differ with them and in so hating expend their force in tearing themselves to pieces.

The safe side lies in calling daily for the thought current of wisdom from the Infinite Mind. When that wisdom is more invoked our "reforms" and organizations "for the good of the whole" will not run into internal wrangles almost as soon as they organize. As now conducted the thought current of hatred of and antagonism to the "oppressor" and monopolist is admitted at their birth. This very force breeds quarrels and dissensions among the members. It is force used to tear down instead of build up. It is like taking the fire used to generate steam in the boilers and scattering it throughout the building.

When people come together and in any way talk out their ill-will towards others they are drawing to themselves with ten-fold power an injurious thought current. Because the more minds united on any purpose the more power do they attract to effect that purpose. The thought current so attracted by those chronic complainers, grumblers and scandal mongers, will injure their bodies. Because whatever thought is most held in mind is most materialized in the body.

If we are always thinking and talking of people's imperfections we are drawing to us ever of that thought current, and thereby incorporating into ourselves those very imperfections. We have said in previous books that "Talk Creates Force," and that the more who talk in sympathy the greater is the volume and power of the thought current generated and attracted for good or ill.

THE MEDIUMSHIP OF SPIRIT

A group of gossips who can never put their heads together without raking over the faults of the absent are unconsciously working a law with terrible results to themselves. Gossip is fascinating. There is an exhilaration in scandal and the raking over of our friend's or neighbor's or enemy's faults is almost equal to that produced by champagne. But in the end we pay dearly for these pleasures.

If but two people were to meet at regular intervals and talk of health, strength and vigor of body and mind, at the same time opening their minds to receive of the Supreme the best idea as to the ways and means for securing these blessings, they would attract to them a thought current of such idea. If these two people or more kept up these conversations on these subjects at a regular time and place, and found pleasure in such communings, and they were not forced or stilted; if they could carry them on without controversy, and enter into them without preconceived idea, and not allow any shade of tattle or tale-bearing, or censure of others to drift into their talk, they would be astonished at the year's end at the beneficial results to mind and body. Because in so doing and coming together with a silent demand of the Supreme to get the best idea, they would attract to them a current of Life-giving force.

Let two so commence rather than more. For even two persons in the proper agreement and accord to bring the desired results are not easy to find. The desire for such meetings must be spontaneous, and any other motive will bar out the highest thought current for good. The old-fashioned revival meeting, or camp meeting, through the combined action and desire of a number of minds brought a thought current, causing for the time the ecstasy, fervor and enthusiasm which characterized those gatherings the Native American Indian worked himself into the frenzy of his war dance by a similar law. He brought to him by force of united desire a thought element and current which stimulated and even intoxicated him. His sole desire was to bring on him this mental intoxication. The more minds so working in the same vein, the quicker came the desired result.

The real orator in his effort draws to him a current of thought, which assent again from him to his audience, thrills them. So does the inspired actor or actress. They bring a higher and more powerful element of thought to themselves first, and this flowing through them acts on the audience afterwards. If you dwell a great deal on your own faults you will by the same laws attract more and more of their thought current, and so increase those faults. It is enough that you recognize in yourself those faults.

Don't be always saying of yourself, "I am weak or cowardly or ill-tempered or imprudent," Draw to yourself rather the thought current of strength, courage, even temper, prudence and all other good qualities. Keep the image of these qualities in mind and you make them a part of yourself.

You have sometimes been beset, absorbed, and even annoyed for days in the thought of the suit of clothes you wanted to buy, the cut, color and fashion of a dress, the selection of a bonnet, or cravat, until you were nothing in thought but clothes, hat, bonnet, dress, cravat or some other detail of life. You may not have been able to make up your mind what you should buy, and have then possibly been tossed about mentally on the billows of indecision for days. You have then got into the thought current of thousands of other minds continually in this mood of thought.

Put your mind in the fire of ill-will, envy or jealousy, and it is scarred, seamed and disfigured, because of an element as real as fire, though invisible, acting on it. All things that are evil and imperfect, such as disagreeable traits of character in others—things unpleasant to hear or look upon should be gotten out of our minds as quickly as possible. Otherwise if dwelt upon, they attract of their thought current. They will then become permanent spiritual fixtures, and these will in time materialize themselves into corresponding physical fixtures.

If we are always keeping in mind the person doing some wrong thing, we are the more apt to do that very thing ourselves. Let us Endeavour, then, with the help of the Supreme Power, to get into the thought current of things that are healthy, natural, strong and beautiful. Let us try to avoid thoughts of disease, of suffering, of deformity, of faultiness.

A field of waving grain or the rolling surf is better to contemplate than to pore over the horrors of a railway accident. We do not realize how much we are depressed physically and mentally by the incessant feast of horrors prepared for us by the daily press. We invoke in their perusal a thought current, filled with things and images of horror and suffering. We bring ourselves in this way in connection and oneness with all other morbid and diseased mind, which lives and revels in this current. It leads not to life, but to disease and death.

Neither others nor yourself are one particle aided by your knowing of every fire, explosion, murder, theft or crime which the newspapers chronicle every twenty-four hours. If we read boots written by cynical, sarcastic minds, who are so warped as to be able to see only the faults of others, and at last unable to see good anywhere, we bring on ourselves their unhealthy thought current, and are one with it. The arrow always tipped with ill-nature and sarcasm is deadliest to him who sends it. In other words, the man who is ever inviting and cultivating this thought current, is inviting the unrest, disease and misfortune it will assuredly bring to him, and when we get too much into his mind we invite similar results.

You may be neat, careful and methodical in your habits, exact and elaborate in your work, yet if you associate closely with those who are careless and slovenly you may find in yourself a tendency to be also careless and slovenly, and a difficulty in resuming and carrying out your former neat, methodical and orderly methods. Because you have not only absorbed of the careless mind, or the mind lacking patience to do anything reposefully, but the fragment of such mind so absorbed is acting as a magnet in attracting to you its like thought current.

When an evil is known it is half cured. Bear in mind when you are in any unpleasant frame of mind that a thought current of such disagreeable mood is acting on you. Bear in mind that you are then one in a sort of electrical connection with many other sickly and morbid minds, all generating and sending unpleasant thought to each other.

The next thing to be done is to pray or demand to get out of this current of evil thought. You cannot do this wholly of your own individual effort. You must demand of the Supreme Power to divert it from you. We can more and more invite the thought current of things that are lively, sprightly and amusing. Life should be full of playfulness. Continued seriousness is but a few degrees removed front gloom and melancholy.

Thousands live too much in the thought current of seriousness. Faces which wear a smiling expression are scarce. Some never smile at all. Some have forgotten how to smile, and it actually hurts them to smile, or to see others do so. Sickness and disease are nursed into fresher and fresher activity by the serious mood of mind. Habit continually strengthens the sad capacity of dwelling on the malady, which may be the merest trifle at first. People get so much in this current that woeful diseases are manufactured out of some trifling irritation in some part of the body.

Many material things are helps to divert a thought current acting disagreeably on you. You may have daily a set of disagreeable symptoms. They may seem to come as adjuncts to the daily routine of life. The breakfast table, the furniture, the conversation and even the persons immediately about you seem to recall them. Travel sometimes banishes them entirely. The sight of different surroundings diverts that particular thought current. Material remedies may temporarily effect the same result. So may any sudden change of life or occupation. But all these are secondary aids to the Supreme Power.

The thought current of fear is everywhere. All humanity fears something–disease, death, loss of fortune, loss of friends, loss of something. Everyone has his or her pet fear. It extends to the most trivial details of life. The streets are full of people who, if fearing nothing else, fear they won't catch a train or the next street car.

The more sensitive you are to the impress of thought, the more liable are you to be affected by this thought current of fear until your spirit, by constant demand of the Supreme Power, builds up for itself an armor of thought positive to this current, and one which will deny it access.

You can commence this building in saying, whenever you are affected in the way above mentioned, or in any disagreeable fashion, "I refuse to accept this thought and the mental condition it has brought on me which affects my body." You commence then to turn aside the thought current of evil.

Everyone has some pet fearsome disease they may never have had, but always dreaded–something they are in special fear of losing. Some trifle, even but a word or sentence uttered by another, brings this pet fear to the mind. Instantly through long habit the minds reverts to this fear. Instantly it opens to it, and the whole thought, volume and current rushes to and acts on them. It acts and vibrates on that particular chord of your nature, which for years has sounded your pet weakness. Then in some way the body is affected disagreeably.

There are myriads of different symptoms. The body may become weak and tremulous. There may be loss of appetite, tremulousness, a dry tongue, a bad taste in the mouth, weakness in the joints, drowsiness, difficulty of concentrating the mind on your business and many other disagreeable sensations. Such symptoms are often classed as "malaria." In a sense the name is a correct one. Only in very many of these cases it is a bad atmosphere or current of thought which is acting on our minds instead of the fancied bad material atmosphere.

Unquestionably an atmosphere full of vegetable or animal decomposition will affect many people. But some live for years in the midst of stagnant pools and swamps who never have malaria. Others far removed from such locations on high and dry ground do have it. They have taken on a thought current of fear.

Place yourself in a house where there has recently been a panic or scare, though you may know nothing of it. You were well and strong the day before. You arise in the morning, and soon this whole train of disagreeable sensations affects you, because the house or place is saturated with a thought current of fear.

Put a fear on city, town or country of some deadly epidemic or some great calamity, and hundreds of the more sensitive who may have no fear of that epidemic or calamity are still affected by it disagreeably. That thought current affects them in their particular a weak spot. A fanatic predicts some great catastrophe.

The sensational newspapers take up the topic, ventilate it, affect to ridicule, but still write about it. This sets more minds to thinking and more people to talking. The more talk the more of this injurious force is generated. As a result thousands of people are affected by it unpleasantly, some in one way, some in another, because the whole force of that volume of fear is let loose upon them. Some are killed outright. Entirely unaware of the cause, they open their minds more and more to it, dwell on it in secret, put out no resisting thought until at last the spirit, unable longer to carry such a load, snaps the link which connects it with the body.

THE MEDIUMSHIP OF SPIRIT

The more impressionable you are to the thought about you the more are you liable to be thus affected. But you can train your mind to shut out this thought. You can gradually train it to bar tightly this door to weakness, and keep open only the one to strength. You can do this by cultivating the mood of drawing to yourself and keeping in the mood and current of thought coming of God or the Supreme Power for good. Impressionability or capacity to receive thought is source either of strength or weakness.

Fine-grained, sensitive, highly developed minds today often carry the weakest bodies, because through ignorance they are always inviting some of these currents of evil without any knowledge of their existence or the means of throwing them off. They are ignorantly either courting or exposing themselves to such current. Improper individual association is one chief source of such exposure.

As you place your reliance on the Infinite Mind to bring you out of all these agencies for ill, that mind in some way will bring many material aids to help you out. That mind will suggest medicines and foods and surroundings and changes, not only to help you temporarily, but permanently, so that when you are cured you are cured for all time.

A cheerful, buoyant, hopeful mind (and no mind is cheerful, hopeful and buoyant without being nearer the Infinite than one that is depressed, sour and gloomy), be that the mind of your doctor, or your friend, will help you to get out of the injurious thought current. Regard such mind as a help from the Infinite. But don't put your whole trust in that individual. Put the great trust in the Supreme Power which has sent to you the individual as a temporary aid or crutch until your spiritual limbs are strong enough to bear you.

The more you get into the thought current coming from the Infinite Mind, making yourself more and more a part of that mind (exactly as you may become a part of any vein of low, morbid, unhealthy mind in opening yourself to that current), the quicker are you freshened, and renewed physically and mentally. You become continually a newer being. Changes for the better come quicker and quicker. Your power increases to bring results.

You lose gradually all fear as it is proven more and more to you that when you are in the thought current of Infinite good there is nothing to fear. You realize more and more clearly that there is a great power and force which cares for you. You are wonderstruck at the fact that when your mind is set in the right direction all material things come to you with very little physical or external effort.

You wonder then at man's toiling and striving, working himself literally to death, when through such excess of effort he actually drives from him the rounded-out good of health, happiness and material prosperity all combined. You will see in this demand for the highest good that you are growing to power greater than you ever dreamed of.

It will dawn on you that the real life destined for the awakened few now, and the many in the future is a dazzling dream—a permanent realization that it is a happiness to exist—a serenity and contentment without abatement—a transition from pleasure to pleasure, and from the great to the greater pleasure.

You find as you get more and more into the current of the Infinite Mind that exhausting toil is not required of you, but that when you commit yourself in trust to this current and let it bear you where it will, all things needful will come to you.

When you are getting into the right thought current, you may for a time experience more of uneasiness, physical and mental than ever. This is because the new element acting on you makes you more sensitive to the presence of evil. The new is driving the old out. The new thought current searches and detects every little error in your mind before unnoticed, and repels it. This causes a struggle, and mind and body are for a time unpleasantly affected by it.

It is like house-cleaning, a process usually involving a good deal of dust and disturbance. The new spirit you call to you is cleaning your spiritual house. There is no limit to the power of the thought current you can attract to you nor limit to the things that can he done through the individual by it. In the future some people will draw so much of the higher quality of thought to them, that by it they will accomplish what some would call miracles. In this capacity of the human mind for drawing a thought current ever increasing in fineness of quality and power lies the secret of what has been called "magic."

TWELVE - How To Use Your Thought Energies

GENERALLY speaking, we may say that the power of mind is the sum-total of all the forces of the mental world, including those forces that are employed in the process of thinking. Your thought energies includes the power of the will, the power of desire, the power of feeling, and the power of thought. It includes conscious action in all its phases and subconscious action in all its phases; in fact, it includes anything and everything that is placed in action through the mind, by the mind or in the mind.

To use your thought energies, the first essential is to direct every mental action toward the goal in view, and this direction must not be occasional, but constant. Most minds, however, do not apply this law. They think about a certain thing one moment, and about something else the next moment. At a certain hour their mental actions work along a certain line, and at the next hour those actions work along a different line.

Sometimes the goal in view is one thing, and sometimes another, so the actions of the mind do not move constantly toward a certain definite goal, but are mostly scattered. We know, however, that every individual who is actually working themselves steadily and surely toward the goal they have in view, invariably directs all the power of their thought upon that goal. In their mind not a single mental action is thrown away, not a single mental force wasted. All the power that is in them is being directed to work for what they wish to accomplish, and the reason that every power responds in this way is because they are not thinking of one thing now and something else the next moment. They are thinking all the time of what they wish to attain and achieve. The full power of mind is turned upon that object, and as mind is the ruling power, the full power of all their other forces will tend to work for the same object.

In using the power of mind as well as all the other forces we possess, the first question to answer is what we really want, or what we really want to accomplish; and when this question is answered, the one thing that is wanted should be fixed so clearly in thought that it can be seen by the mind's eye every minute.

But the majority do not know what they really want. They may have some vague desire, but they have not determined clearly, definitely and positively what they really want, and this is one of the principal causes of

78

failure. So long as we do not know definitely what we want, our forces will be scattered, and so long as our forces are scattered, we will accomplish but little, or fail entirely.

When we know what we want, however, and proceed to work for it with all the power and ability that is in us, we may rest assured that we will get it. When we direct the power of thinking, the power of will, the power of mental action, the power of desire, the power of ambition, in fact, all the power we possess on the one thing we want, on the one goal we desire to reach, it is not difficult to understand why success in a greater and greater measure must be realized.

To illustrate this subject further, we will suppose that you have a certain ambition and continue to concentrate your thought and the power of your mind upon that ambition every minute for an indefinite period, with no cessation whatever. The result will be that you will gradually and surely train all the forces within you to work for the realization of that ambition, and in the course of time, the full capacity of your entire mental system will be applied in working for that particular thing.

On the other hand, suppose you do as most people do under average circumstances. Suppose, after you have given your ambition a certain amount of thought, you come to the conclusion that possibly you might succeed better along another line. Then you begin to direct the power of your mind along that other line. Later on, you come to the conclusion that there is still another channel through which you might succeed, and you proceed accordingly to direct your mind upon this third ambition. Then what will happen? Simply this: You will make three good beginnings, but in every case you will stop before you have accomplished anything.

There are thousands of capable men and women, however, who make this mistake every year of their lives. The full force of their mental system is directed upon a certain ambition only for a short time; then it is directed elsewhere. They never continue long enough along any particular line to secure results from their efforts, and therefore results are never secured.

Then there are other minds who give most of their attention to a certain ambition and succeed fairly well, but give the rest of their attention to a number of minor ambitions that have no particular importance. Thus they are using only a fraction of their power in a way that will tell. The rest of it is thrown away along a number of lines through which nothing is gained.

But in this age efficiency is demanded everywhere in world's work, and anyone who wants to occupy a place that will satisfy their ambition and desire, cannot afford to waste even a small part of the power they may possess. They need it all along the line of their leading ambition, and therefore should not permit counter attractions to occupy their mind for a moment.

If you have a certain ambition or a certain desire, think about that ambition at all times. Keep that ambition before your mind constantly, and do not hesitate to make your ambition as high as possible. The higher you aim, the greater will be your achievements, though that does not necessarily mean that you will realize your highest aims as fully as you have pictured them in your mind; but the fact is that those who have low aims, usually realize what is even below their aims, while those who have high aims usually realize very nearly, if not fully, what their original ambition calls for.

The principle is to direct your thought energies upon the very highest, the very largest and the very greatest mental conception of that which we intend to achieve. The first essential therefore, is to direct the full power of mind and thought upon the goal in view, and to continue to direct the mind in that manner every minute, regardless of circumstances or conditions. The second essential is to make every mental action positive.

When we desire certain things or when we think of certain things we wish to attain or achieve, the question should be if our mental attitudes at the time are positive or negative. To answer this we only have to remember that every positive action always goes toward that which receives its attention, while a negative action always retreats. A positive action is an action that you feel when you realize that every force in your entire system is pushed forward, so to speak, and that it is passing through what may be termed an expanding and enlarging state of feeling or consciousness.

The positive attitude of mind is also indicated by the feeling of a firm, determined fullness throughout the nervous system. When every nerve feels full, strong and determined, you are in the positive attitude, and whatever you may do at the time will produce results along the line of your desire or your ambition. When you are in a positive state of mind you are never nervous or disturbed, you are never agitated or strenuous; in fact, the more positive you are the deeper your calmness and the better your control over your entire system.

The positive man is not one who rushes helter-skelter here and there regardless of judgment or constructive action, but one who is absolutely calm and controlled under every circumstance, and yet so thoroughly full of energy that every atom in his being is ready, under every circumstance, to accomplish and achieve.

This energy is not permitted to act, however, until the proper time arrives, and then its action goes directly to the goal in view. The positive mind is always in harmony with itself, while the negative mind is always out of harmony, and thereby loses the greater part of its power. Positiveness always means strength stored up, power held in the system under perfect control, until the time of action; and during the time of action directed constructively under the same perfect control.

In the positive mind, all the actions of the mental system are working in harmony and are being fully directed toward the object in view, while in the negative mind, those same actions are scattered, restless, nervous, disturbed, moving here and there, sometimes under direction, but most of the time not.

That the one should invariably succeed is therefore just as evident as that the other should invariably fail. Scattered energy cannot do otherwise but fail, while positively directed energy simply must succeed. A positive mind is like a powerful stream of water that is gathering volume and force from hundreds of tributaries all along its course.

The further on it goes the greater its power, until when it reaches its goal, that power is simply immense. A negative mind, however, would be something like a stream, that the further it flows the more divisions it makes, until, when it reaches its goal, instead of being one powerful stream, it has become a hundred small, weak, shallow streams.

To develop positiveness it is necessary to cultivate those qualities that constitute positiveness. Make it a point to give your whole attention to what you want to accomplish, and give that attention firmness, calmness and determination. Try to give depth to every desire until you feel as if all the powers of your system were acting, not on the surface, but from the greater world within. As this attitude is cultivated, positiveness will become more and more distinct, until you can actually feel yourself gaining power and prestige.

And the effect will not only be noticed in your own ability to better direct and apply your talents, but others will discover the change. Accordingly, those who are looking for people of power, people who can do things, will look to you as the one to occupy the position that has to be filled.

Positiveness therefore, not only gives you the ability to make a far better use of the forces you possess, but it also gives you personality, that much admired something that will most surely cause you to be selected where people of power are needed. The world does not care for negative personalities.

Such personalities look weak and empty, and are usually ignored, but everybody is attracted to a positive personality; and it is the positive personality that is always given the preference. Nor is this otherwise but right, because the positive personality has better use of their power, and therefore is able to act with greater efficiency wherever they are called upon to act.

The third essential in the right use of the mind is to make every mental action constructive, and a constructive mental action is one that is based upon a deep seated desire to develop, to increase, to achieve, to attain – in brief, to become larger and greater, and to do something of far greater worth than has been done before.

If you will cause every mental action you entertain to have that feeling, constructiveness will soon became second nature to your entire mental system; that is, all the forces of your mind will begin to become building forces, and will continue to build you up along any line through which you may desire to act.

Inspire your mind constantly with a building desire, and make this desire so strong that very part of your system will constantly feel that it wants to become greater, more capable and more efficient. An excellent practice in this connection is to try to enlarge upon all your ideas of things whenever you have spare moments for real thought.

This practice will tend to produce a growing tendency in every process of your thinking. Another good practice is to inspire every mental action with more ambition. We cannot have too much ambition. We may have too much aimless ambition, but we cannot have too much real constructive ambition. If your ambition is very strong, and is directed toward something definite, every action of your mind, every action of your personality, and every action of your faculties will become constructive; that is, all those actions will be inspired by the tremendous force of your ambition to work for the realization of that ambition.

Never permit restless ambition. Whenever you feel the force of ambition, direct your mind at once in a calm, determined manner upon that which you really want to accomplish in life. Make this a daily practice, and you will steadily train all your faculties and powers not only to work for the realization of that ambition, but become more and more efficient in that direction. Before long your forces and faculties will be sufficiently competent to accomplish what you want.

In the proper use of the mind therefore, these three essentials should be applied constantly and thoroughly. First, direct all the powers of mind, all the powers of thought, and all your thinking upon the goal you have in view. Second, train every mental action to be deeply and calmly positive. Third, train every mental action to be constructive, to be filled with a building spirit, to be inspired with a ceaseless desire to develop the greater, to achieve the greater, to attain the greater.

When you have acquired these three, you will begin to use your forces in such a way that results must follow. You will begin to move forward steadily and surely, and you will be constantly gaining ground. Your mind will have become like the stream mentioned above. It will gather volume and force as it moves on and on, until finally that volume will be great enough to remove any obstacle in its way, and that force powerful enough to do anything you may have in view.

In order to apply these three essentials in the most effective manner, there are several misuses of the mind that must be avoided. Avoid the forceful, the aggressive, and the domineering attitudes, and do not permit your mind to become intense, unless it is under perfect control. Never attempt to control or influence others in any way whatever. You will seldom succeed in that manner, and when you do, the success will be temporary; besides, such a practice always weakens your mind.

Do not turn the power of your mind upon others, but turn it upon yourself in such a way that it will make you stronger, more positive, more capable, and more efficient, and as you develop in this manner, success must come of itself. There is only one way by which you can influence others legitimately and that is through the giving of instruction, but in that case, there is no desire to influence. You desire simply to impart knowledge and information, and you exercise a most desirable influence without desiring to do so.

A great many men and women, after discovering the immense power of mind, have come to the conclusion that they might change circumstances by exercising mental power upon those circumstances in some mysterious manner, but such a practice means nothing but a waste of energy. The way to control circumstances is to control the forces within yourself to make a greater human being of yourself, and as you become greater and more competent, you will naturally gravitate into better circumstances. In this connection, we should remember that like attracts like.

If you want that which is better, make yourself better. If you want to realize the ideal, make yourself more ideal. If you want better friends, make yourself a better friend. If you want to associate with people of worth, make yourself more worthy. If you want to meet that which is agreeable, make yourself more agreeable. If you want to enter conditions and circumstances that are more pleasing, make yourself more pleasing. In brief, whatever you want, produce that something in yourself, and you will positively gravitate towards the corresponding conditions in the external world.

But to improve yourself along those lines, it is necessary to apply for that purpose, all the power you possess. You cannot afford to waste any of it, and every misuse of the mind will waste power. Avoid all destructive attitudes of the mind, such an anger, hatred, malice, envy, jealousy, revenge, depression, discouragement, disappointment, worry, fear, and so on. Never antagonize, never resist what is wrong, and never try to get even.

THE MEDIUMSHIP OF SPIRIT

Make the best use of your own talent and the best that is in store for you will positively come your way. When others seem to take advantage of you, do not retaliate by trying to take advantage of them. Use your power in improving yourself, so that you can do better and better work. That is how you are going to win in the race.

Later on, those who tried to take advantage of you will be left in the rear. Remember, those who are dealing unjustly with you or with anybody are misusing their mind. They are therefore losing their power, and will, in the course of time, begin to lose ground; but if you, in the mean time, are turning the full power of your mind to good account, you will not only gain more power, but you will soon begin to gain ground.

You will gain and continue to gain in the long run, while others who have been misusing their minds will lose mostly everything in the long run. That is how you are going to win, and win splendidly regardless of ill treatment or opposition.

A great many people imagine that they can promote their own success by trying to prevent the success of other, but it is one of the greatest delusions in the world. If you want to promote your own success as thoroughly as your capacity will permit, take an active interest in the success of everybody, because this will not only keep your mind in the success attitude and cause you to think success all along the line, but it will enlarge your mind so as to give you a greater and better grasp upon the fields of success.

If you are trying to prevent the success of others, you are acting in the destructive attitude, which sooner or later will react on others, but if you are taking an active interest in the success of everybody, you are entertaining only constructive attitudes, and these will sooner or later accumulate in your own mind to add volume and power to the forces of success that you are building up in yourself.

In this connection, we may well ask why those succeed who do succeed, why so many succeed only in part, and why so many fail utterly. These are questions that occupy the minds of most people, and hundreds of answers have been given, but there is only one answer that goes to rock bottom. Those people who fail, and who continue to fail all along the line, fail because the power of their minds is either in a habitual negative state, or is always misdirected. If the power of mind is not working positively and constructively for a certain goal, you are not going to succeed. If your mind is not positive, it is negative, and negative minds float with the stream.

We must remember that we are in the midst of all kinds of circumstances, some of which are for us and some of which are against us, and we will either have to make our own way or drift, and if we drift we go wherever the stream goes. But most of the streams of human life are found to float in the world of the ordinary and the inferior. Therefore, if you drift, you will drift with the inferior, and your goal will be failure.

When we analyze the minds of people who have failed, we invariably find that they are either negative, non-constructive or aimless. Their forces are scattered, and what is in them is seldom applied constructively. There is an emptiness about their personality that indicates negativeness. There is an uncertainty in their facial expression that indicates the absence of definite ambition. There is nothing of a positive, determined nature going on in their mental world.

They have not taken definite action along any line. They are dependent upon fate and circumstances. They are drifting with some stream, and that they should accomplish little if anything is inevitable. This does not mean, however, that their mental world is necessarily unproductive; in fact, those very minds are in many instances immensely rich with possibilities. The trouble is, those possibilities continue to be dormant, and what is in them is not being brought forth and trained for definite action or actual results.

What these people should do, is to proceed at once to comply with the three essentials mentioned above, and before many months there will be a turn in the lane. They will soon cease to drift, and will then begin to make their own life, their own circumstances, and their own future.

In this connection, it is well to remember that negative people and non-constructive minds never attract that which is helpful in their circumstances. The more you drift, the more people you meet who also drift, while on the other hand, when you begin to make your own life and become positive, you begin to meet more positive people and more constructive circumstances. This explains why "God helps them that help themselves."

THE MEDIUMSHIP OF SPIRIT

When you begin to help yourself, which means to make the best of what is in yourself, you begin to attract to yourself more and more of those helpful things that may exist all about you. In other words, constructive forces attract constructive forces; positive forces attract positive forces. A growing mind attracts elements and forces that help to promote growth, and people who are determined to make more and more of themselves, are drawn more and more into circumstances through which they will find the opportunity to make more of themselves. And this law works not only in connection with the external world, but also the internal world.

When you begin to make a positive determined use of those powers in yourself that are already in Positive action, you draw forth into action powers within you that have been dormant, and as this process continues, you will find that you will accumulate volume, capacity and power in your mental world, until you finally become a mental giant.

As you begin to grow and become more capable, you will find that you will meet better and better opportunities, not only opportunities for promoting external success, but opportunities for further building yourself up along the lines of ability, capacity and talent. You thus demonstrate the law that "Nothing succeeds like success," and "To him that hath shall be given." And here it is well to remember that it is not necessary to possess external things in the beginning to be counted among them "that hath.." It is only necessary in the beginning to possess the interior riches; that is, to take control of what is in you, and proceed to use it positively with a definite goal in view.

He who has control of his own mind has already great riches. He has sufficient wealth to be placed among those who have. He is already successful, and if he continues as he has begun, his success will soon appear in the external world. Thus the wealth that existed at first in the internal only will take shape and form in the external. This is a law that is unfailing, and there is not a man or woman on the face of the earth that cannot apply it with the most satisfying results.

The reason why so many fail is thus found in the fact that they do not fully and constructively apply the forces and powers they possess, and the reason why so many succeed only to a slight degree is found in the fact that only a small fraction of their power is applied properly. The reason why those succeed who do succeed is found in the fact that a large measure of their forces and powers is applied according to those three essentials, and as those essentials can be applied by anyone, even to the most perfect degree, there is no reason why all should not succeed.

Sometimes we meet people who have only ordinary ability, but who are very successful. Then we meet others who have great ability but who are not successful, or who succeed only to a slight degree. At first we see no explanation, but when we understand the cause of success as well as the cause of failure, the desired explanation is easily found. The man or woman with ordinary ability, if they comply with the three essentials necessary to the right use of mind, will naturally succeed, though if they had greater ability, their success would of course become greater in proportion. But the individual who has great ability, yet does not apply the three essentials necessary to the right use of mind, cannot succeed.

The positive and constructive use of the power of mind, with a definite goal in view will invariably result in advancement, attainment and achievement, but if we wish to use that power in its full capacity, the action of the mind must be deep. In addition to the right use of the mind, we must also learn the full use of mind, and as the full use implies the use of the whole mind, the deeper mental fields and forces, as well as the usual mental fields and forces, it is necessary to understand the subconscious as well as the conscious.

In using the power of the mind, the deeper the action of thought, will and desire, the greater the result. Accordingly, all mental action to be strong and effective, must be subconscious; that is, it must act in the field of the mental undercurrent as it is in this field that things are actually done. Those forces that play upon the surface of mind may be changed and turned from their course by almost any outside influence, and their purpose thus averted. But this is never true of the undercurrents.

Anything that gets into the mental undercurrents will be seen through to a finish, regardless of external circumstances or conditions; and it is with difficulty that the course of these currents is changed when once they have been placed in full positive action.

It is highly important therefore that we permit nothing to take action in these undercurrents that we do not wish to encourage and promote; and for the same reason, it is equally important that we cause everything to take action in these currents that we do wish to encourage and promote. These undercurrents, however, act only through the subconscious, and are controlled by the subconscious. In consequence, it is the subconscious which we must understand and act upon if we want the power of mind to work with full capacity and produce the greatest measure possible of the results desired.

In defining the subconscious mind, it is first necessary to state that it is not a separate mind. There are not two minds. There is only one mind in man, but it has two phases – the conscious and the subconscious. We may define the conscious as the upper side of the mentality, and the subconscious as the underside. The subconscious may also be defined as a vast mental field permeating the entire objective personality, thereby filling every atom of the personality through and through.

We shall come nearer the truth, however, if we think of the subconscious as a finer mental force, having distinct powers, functions and possibilities, or as a great mental sea of life, energy and power, the force and capacity of which has never been measured. The conscious mind is on the surface, and therefore we act through the conscious mind whenever mental action moves through the surface of thought, will or desire, but whenever we enter into deeper mental action and sound the vast depths of this underlying mental life, we touch the subconscious, though we must remember that we do not become oblivious to the conscious every time we touch the subconscious, as the two are inseparably united.

That the two phases of the mind are related can be well illustrated by comparing the conscious mind with a sponge, and the subconscious with the water permeating the sponge. We know that every fiber of the sponge is in touch with the water, and in the same manner, every part of the conscious mind, as well as every atom in the personality, is in touch with the subconscious, and completely filled, through and through, with the life and the force of the subconscious.

It has frequently been stated that the subconscious mind occupies the Fourth Dimension of space, and though this is a matter that cannot be exactly demonstrated, nevertheless, the more we study the nature of the subconscious, as well as the Fourth Dimension, the more convinced we become that the former occupies the field of the latter. This, however, is simply a matter that holds interest in philosophical investigation. Whether the subconscious occupies the Fourth Dimension or some other dimension of space will make no difference as to its practical value.

In order to understand the subconscious, it is well at the outset to familiarize ourselves with its natural functions, as this will convince ourselves of the fact that we are not dealing with something that is beyond normal mental action.

The subconscious mind controls all the natural functions of the body, such as the circulation, respiration, digestion, assimilation, physical repair, etc. It also controls all the involuntary actions of the body, and all those actions of mind and body that continue their natural movements without direction from the will. The subconscious perpetuates characteristics, traits, and qualities that are peculiar to individuals, species and races. What is called heredity therefore is altogether a subconscious process. The same is true of what is called second nature.

Whenever anything has been repeated a sufficient number of times to have become habitual, it becomes second nature, or rather a subconscious action. It frequently happens, however, that a conscious action may become a subconscious action without repetition, and thus becomes second nature almost at once.

When we examine the nature of the subconscious, we find that it responds to almost anything the conscious mind may desire or direct, though it is usually necessary for the conscious mind to express its desire upon the subconscious for some time before the desired response is secured. The subconscious is a most willing servant, and is so competent that thus far we have failed to find a single thing along mental lines that it will not or cannot do. It submits readily to almost any kind of training, and will do practically anything that it is directed to do, whether the thing is to our advantage or not.

In this connection, it is interesting to learn that there are a number of things in the human system usually looked upon as natural, and inevitable, that are simply the results of misdirected subconscious training in the past. We frequently speak of human weaknesses as natural, but weakness is never natural. Although it may appear, it is invariably the result of imperfect subconscious training. It is never natural to go wrong, but it is natural to go right, and the reason why is simple.

THE MEDIUMSHIP OF SPIRIT

Every right action is in harmony with natural law, while every wrong action is a violation of natural law. It has also been stated that the aging process is natural, but modern science has demonstrated that it is not natural for a person to age at sixty, seventy, or eighty years. The fact that the average person does manifest nearly all the conditions of old age at those periods of time, or earlier, simply proves that the subconscious mind has been trained through many generations to produce old age at sixty, seventy, eighty or ninety, as the case may be, and the subconscious always does what it has been trained to do.

It can just as readily be trained, however, to produce greater physical strength and greater mental capacity at ninety than we possess at thirty or forty. It can also be trained to possess the same virile youth at one hundred as the healthiest man or woman of twenty may possess. In fact, practically every condition that appears in the mind, the character and the personality of the human race, is the result of what the subconscious mind has been directed to do during past generations.

It is therefore evident that as the subconscious is directed to produce different conditions in mind, character, and personality – conditions that are in perfect harmony with the natural law of human development, such conditions will invariably appear in the race. Thus we understand how a new race or a superior race may appear upon this planet.

There are a great many people who are disturbed over the fact that they have inherited certain characteristics or ailments from their parents, but what they have inherited is simply subconscious tendencies in that direction, and those tendencies can be changed absolutely. What we inherit from our parents can be eliminated so completely that no one would ever know it had been there. In like manner, we can improve so decidedly upon the good qualities that we have inherited from our parents that any similarity between parent and child in those respects would disappear completely.

The subconscious mind is always ready, willing and competent to make any change for the better in our physical or mental make-up that we may desire, though it does not work in some miraculous manner, nor does it usually produce results instantaneously. In most instances its actions are gradual, but they invariably produce the results intended if the proper training continues. The subconscious mind will respond to the directions of

91

the conscious mind so long as those directions do not interfere with the absolute laws of nature.

The subconscious never moves against natural law, but it has the power to so use natural law that improvement along any line can be secured. It will reproduce in mind and body any condition that is thoroughly impressed and deeply felt by the conscious mind. It will bring forth undesirable conditions when directed to produce such conditions, and it will bring forth health, strength, youth and added power when so directed.

If you continue to desire a strong physical body, and fully expect the subconscious to build for you a stronger body, you will find that this will gradually or finally be done. You will steadily grow in physical strength. If you continue to desire greater ability along a certain line and expect the subconscious to produce greater mental power along that line, your ability will increase as expected, but it is necessary in this connection to be persistent and persevering. To become enthusiastic about these things for a few days is not sufficient. It is when we apply these laws persistently for weeks, months and years that we find the results to be, not only what we expected, but frequently far greater.

Everything has a tendency to grow in the subconscious. Whenever an impression or desire is placed in the subconscious, it has a tendency to become larger and therefore the bad becomes worse when it enters the subconscious, while the good becomes better. We have the power, however, to exclude the bad from the subconscious and cause only the good to enter that immense field.

Whenever you say that you are tired and permit that feeling to sink into the subconscious, you will almost at once feel more tired. Whenever you feel sick and permit that feeling to enter the subconscious, you always feel worse. The same is true when you are weak, sad, disappointed or depressed. If you let those feelings sink into your subconscious, they will become worse.

On the other hand, when we feel happy, strong, persistent and determined, and permit those feelings to enter the subconscious, we always feel better. It is therefore highly important that we positively refuse to give in to any undesirable feeling. Whenever we give in to any feeling, it becomes subconscious, and if that feeling is bad, it becomes worse; but so long as we keep undesirable feelings on the outside, so to speak, we will hold them at bay, until nature can readjust itself or gather reserve force and thus put them out of the way altogether.

We should never give in to sickness, though that does not mean that we should continue to work as hard as usual when not feeling well, or cause mind and body to continue in their usual activities. When we find it necessary, we should give ourselves a complete rest, but we should never give in to the feeling of sickness.

The rest that may be taken will help the body to recuperate, and when it does the threatening ailment will disappear. When you feel tired or depressed, do not admit it, but turn your attention at once upon something that is extremely interesting -- something that will completely turn your mind towards the pleasing, the more desirable or the ideal. Persist in feeling the way you want to feel, and permit only wholesome feelings to enter the subconscious. Thus wholesome feelings will live and grow, and after awhile your power to feel good at all times will have become so strong that you can put out of the way any adverse feeling that may threaten at any time.

In this connection, we may mention something that holds more than usual interest. It has been stated by those who are in a position to know, that no one dies until they give up; that is, gives in to those adverse conditions that are at work in their system, tending to produce physical death. So long as he or she refuses to give in to those conditions, they continue to live.

How long a person could refuse to give in even under the most adverse circumstances is a question, but one thing is certain, that thousands and thousands of deaths could be prevented every year if the patient in each case refused to give in. In many instances, the forces of life and death are almost equally balanced.

Which one is going to win depends upon the mental attitude of the patient. If he or she gives over the mind and will to the side of the forces of life, those forces are most likely to win, but if they permit the mind to act with death, the forces of death are most certain to win. So long as one continues to persist in living, refusing absolutely to give into death, they are throwing the full power of mind, thought and will on the side of life. They thereby increase the power of life, and may increase that power sufficiently to overcome death. Again we say that it is a question how many times a person could overcome death by this method, but the fact remains that this method alone can save life repeatedly in the majority of cases; and all will admit after further thought on this subject that the majority will be very large.

This is a method, therefore, that deserves the best of attention in every sickroom. No person should be permitted to die until all available methods for prolonging life have been exhausted, and this last mentioned method is one that will accomplish far more than most of us may expect; and its secret is found in the fact that whenever we give in to any condition or action, it becomes stronger, due to the tendency of the subconscious to enlarge, increase and magnify whatever it receives.

Give in to the forces of death, and the subconscious mind will increase the powers of that force. Give in to the forces of life, and the subconscious mind will increase the power of your life and you will continue to live.

Concerning the general possibilities of the subconscious, we should remember that every faculty has a subconscious side, and that it becomes larger and more competent as this subconscious side is developed. This being true, it is evident that ability and genius might be developed in any mind even to a remarkable degree, as no limit has been found to the subconscious in any of its forces. In like manner, every cell in the body has a subconscious side, and therefore, if the subconscious side of the personality were developed, we can realize what improvement would become possible in that field.

There is a subconscious side to all the faculties in human nature, and if these were developed, we understand how man could become ideal, even far beyond our present dreams of a new race. It is not well however to give the major portion of our attention to future possibilities. It is what is possible now that we should aim to develop and apply, and present possibilities indicate that improvement along any line, whether it be in working capacity, ability, health, happiness and character can be secured without fail if the subconscious is properly directed.

THE MEDIUMSHIP OF SPIRIT

To direct the subconscious along any line, it is only necessary to desire what you want and to make those desires so deep and so persistent that they become positive forces in the subconscious field. When you feel that you want a certain thing, give in to that feeling and also make that feeling positive. Give in to your ambitions in the same manner, and also to every desire that you wish to realize. Let your thought of all those things that you wish to increase in any line get into your system, because whatever gets into your system, the subconscious will proceed to develop, work out and express.

In using the subconscious, we should remember that we are not using something that is separated from normal life. The difference between the individual who makes scientific use of the subconscious and the one who does not, is simply this; the latter employs only a small part of their mind, while the former employs the whole of their mind. And this explains why those who employ the subconscious intelligently have greater working capacity, greater ability and greater endurance. In consequence they sometimes do the work of two or three people, and do excellent work in addition. To train the subconscious for practical action is therefore a matter of common sense. It is a matter of refusing to cultivate only a small corner of your mental field when you can cultivate the entire field.

THIRTEEN - Vibrating To A Higher Order

IT has been said that in order for you to get what you want you have to vibrate to it. How does this vibration work? In order to vibrate to something you must have positive thoughts. If you don't, you won't get what you are striving for.

When you are in a positive frame of mind, you will vibrate toward what you wish to achieve. If you have any slight negativity, worry, or are unsure in the slightest degree, this doubting or negative energy can inhibit you from accomplishing your task, unless you stop them immediately and focus on positive thoughts.

Let's say you are looking to get a million dollars. You visualize a check for that amount coming to you. The only problem is you have a slight doubt in your mind you will get it. What will happen? Nothing. You won't get it because you did not vibrate to it. You did not hold the belief that you would get it and did not have a positive attitude about it.

The premise here is that if you aren't sure you want something and you have slight doubts about it, you won't get it because you are not in vibration to it. You are focusing on what you do not want instead of on what you do want.

The Law of Vibration starts that everything in life moves or vibrates. There is nothing that sits idle, even for a second. Everything in life is in a constant state of motion. Look in a microscope at an atom and you will see protons and electrons moving in a circle around a neutron. No matter what it is, it is energy and energy is in constant motion.

Everything that vibrates does so at a certain rate. This rate is known as its frequency. The higher the frequency, the more potent the force will be. Thought is considered the highest form of vibration therefore it has the highest frequency. Being the highest frequency, it is considered as a powerful force in the universe.

To understand the Law of Attraction correctly, and be in more harmony with it, we must also understand the Law of Vibration. The meaning of vibration can be considered as a moving backwards and forwards. It also can mean to oscillate, quiver, or swing. A perfect way to rationalize on this concept, think about this. If you stick your arm out straight and keep it perfectly still, you will notice no movement. You will notice your arm not moving, but what you don't realize is that under that skin of your arm, the electrons that are contained therein are moving on a steady basis. And they are moving at a speed of about 186,300 miles per second.

Although the arm appears still, it really is in a constant state of motion. You can't see this happening because your eyes can't pick up such minute particles of matter. You can only see this happening if you had a powerful microscope to view it.

Now take a second and vibrate or shake your arm around. Your arm was already vibrating on its own, but you have stepped up the vibration or assisted it to become stronger. The vibrating energy of your arm has increased dramatically.

Those who think positively are in a good state of vibration. Because they are in a good or positive state of vibration, good things will always come to them.

They will always attract positive things or personalities. But those thinking negative would be vibrating negative energy. This is because they dwell on the bad and all that is pessimistic. As such, they will vibrate negativity. And because they vibrate negativity, they will attract anything negative in their lives. This means they will attract trouble, anguish, fear, rage, or whatever negative emotion is available.

If you want to control the results you get, you must control what you vibrate to. This means controlling your thoughts because you only vibrate to the thoughts you have. If you don't get what you want in your life, this is because you are ignorant of what you want. Or you are ignorant to the Law of Vibration.

In electronics, there are electromagnetic fields. If there are two electromagnetic fields working together, they are working in harmony or in resonance. When this occurs, the vibrating rate can easily be transferred from one to the other by way of electrons. The best way to describe this is by providing an example. Let's say you have a glass sitting on a table. There is a lady singing nearby. She hits a certain high note that cracks the glass;

but no other note cracked that glass. Only that one frequency cracked it because the two frequencies were in resonance. The frequency of the lady's voice was the same as the frequency of the magnetic field surrounding the glass.

The same thing happens to your thoughts. When you think of something, and vibrate to it, you are creating a frequency. That frequency goes out into the universe and reaches an object that also vibrates at that same frequency. When this happens, the two are in synch. The electromagnetic waves your brain creates from your thoughts vibrate to the exact energy level as the thing or object that is in the universe you ask for. By concentrating on these though patterns, you increase the energy level of those thoughts and therefore the thoughts become more potent.

What about gratitude? Are you grateful for what you have in your life? Do you acknowledge that every day when you wake up in the morning? The Law of Attraction also includes the Law of Gratitude.

By having the Law of Gratitude, you believe firmly that the Universe is there to give you what you want when you ask for it, that you deserve what you get. You relate to what you have and act in accord to it.

People who lack gratitude always seem to find themselves living in poverty or not having the lifestyle they wish to have. They look upon themselves as lower than anything else and wonder why they can't be better than what they are. The primary reason for this is that they lack acceptance to what they want and do not show to the Universe what they want or deserve to have.

There is no doubt that you get what you ask for and you get it in abundance when you put a lot of effort into it. By showing gratitude, you are showing that the effort you put forth was in tune to what you desired; and you will obtain more of that you wish.

You can tell people by what they have and by what they get just by seeing them and looking at how they dress, walk, and act. You can usually tell if they have gratitude by the way they present themselves. This is why when you look at rich people, you notice they get richer. They have a debt of gratitude and show it every day. This way, they are telling the universe that they are glad they have all these riches and deserve them. The universe responds by giving them more.

If a person does have abundance but does not show gratitude, he will eventually lose it. This is because he is telling the universe that he does not deserve it. When the universe perceives this, the universe stops delivering.

On the other hand, if a person lacks abundance but shows gratitude for what he has, the universe will see that and will in turn give the person more of what that person wishes. This way, that person does not stay in lack for very long.

If a person lacks abundance and does not show gratitude, he will continue to live with lack because he has not shown he deserve more. This is why when we show gratitude, we are closer to the Universe than anyone else. And we get the rewards for doing so. Therefore, the more grateful we are when we get good things, the more good things we will receive. And in some cases, these good things will start coming more rapidly than before. As you create new thoughts and act in harmony with those thoughts with a show of gratitude for having those thoughts, the closer you will be to getting that of which you thought or ask for.

Gratitude has many benefits in that it can keep you from feeling inadequate. It can keep your mind focused on the good rather than the bad. You can think more abundantly by having gratitude. This is why you must obey the Law of Gratitude if you want what you seek.

Think about this. If your show of gratitude is strong, the results that come back to you will be strong. If your debt of gratitude is continuous, your supply will also be continuous. If you start losing your attitude of gratitude, you will find you will lose ground rapidly and end up on the losing end of life. This is why having gratitude is so important. It is so important that it was made into one of the universal laws.

If you think about it, without gratitude, there is a missing link somewhere in our lives. We know that something should be there, but may not realize it until someone points it out. The fact is that saying, "thank you" for what you get is a big step toward having a form of gratitude. But this isn't all there is about the Law of Gratitude. In fact, there is a good definition of the Law of Gratitude that states, "If you are to get the results you seek, it is imperative that you should act on and obey this law." This means that if you do not obey the Law of Gratitude, you will not get what you seek. It is that simple.

Other than being grateful for what you have, what is the exact way that the Law of Gratitude works? It can be stated as a natural principle that action and reaction are equal and opposite in direction at all times. This means that whatever we put our attention or emotional energy on can be good or bad. And this energy will eventually show up in our lives. This is one of the principles you must know and understand. Neither the universe nor our subconscious mind knows good or bad. Both aspects are treated the same. In this regard, what we put our focus on is what we get back.

The importance here is on putting positive energy out to the universe. This way, we are focusing on what we want and not on what we don't want. You may not realize this, but gratitude is very powerful. It has a lot of high-energy positive vibration of thought. Having gratitude intimately connects you to the Universe.

Without gratitude, you have no power, since the two connect together. And by using our minds for positive things, we are in reality using the power we have to produce the reality we want. So when we show gratitude, we are in fact producing high energy positive vibrations of thought. This high energy can only lead to one manifestation – great achievements.

When you do anything in life, you put forth the gratitude to make it work. If you set goals for yourself, you must show gratitude for having accomplished the goals you put down. When you do write your goals down, think of them as having been already achieved and be grateful for them being achieved. Your gratitude will be so powerful, so energized, that people around you can't help but notice that about you.

Those who are not successful or do not get what they want are in fact pushing away the success and are violating the universal law of gratitude. In fact, there are five key mistakes or ways of thinking that people make with gratitude that cause them not to get what they want in life. These five ways include:

THE MEDIUMSHIP OF SPIRIT

1. Abundance: Some people wonder if there is enough to go around for everyone. If your belief that the universe has only a limited supply, you are going nowhere in life and will never amount to anything. This is a major fallacy in life. In fact, there is more than enough abundance in the universe. It is endless. God promised us that we would have abundance forever if we chose to have it. The universe is energy. Energy is everlasting. Therefore, what we want comes from energy. It only goes to show that the universe will never run out of anything we want. It will always supply us with what we want when we want it. We just have to ask.

2. Non-resistance to what is: This is a mistaken thought or principle that people have. It keeps us from having the gratitude we should have. When we think with non-resistance, we are in fact having the mental attitude that whatever happens, happens. We don't fight it, we just let it be. In other words, people who think this way believe they deserve what they got or believe that was the way it was supposed to be. Therefore, they limit themselves to what life has to offer. If it involves something they can't do anything about, they just let it be and state that is the way it was meant to be. In this case, you can apply the law of opposites and think that there is good in the situation instead of bad.

3. No satisfaction: People tend to associate satisfaction with being happy and having abundance. But there is a difference. When you are satisfied, you accept what is. You can be satisfied without being grateful. This is because you accepted things the way they are and not challenge it. Happiness, on the other hand, is a state of joy or gratitude. It is a very positive and attractive mental energy. By being satisfied, you are actually limiting yourself to what you can have in your life. It is important to be happy and satisfied now. It you do, you will have gratitude and will be in the position for much abundance.

4. Forgiveness: You may not know this but forgiveness is also a part of the Law of Gratitude. This means you need to forgive anyone who did bad things to you in the past and even in the present, as well as in the future. This is especially true if you have a grudge against someone for a long time. The way you know you forgive them is by asking yourself if you can either wish them well or be grateful for them. If you can truthfully answer "yes," you have indeed forgiven them. Forgiveness is so vital to our dreams in life that if we don't do it and hold any resentment, fear, or any frustration inside, it can literally block us from getting what we want in life.

Lastly, we must learn to forgive ourselves for what we do to others and our own selves. If we can look at ourselves in the mirror and say we love ourselves, we are on our way to experiencing the life we want.

5. Stop thinking: Unfortunately, people want to stop thinking after they get a thought in their head. They don't want to go beyond thinking and act on what they think. They go into the steps of thinking, but they never act on what they think. Therefore, the key to having gratitude is by acting out what you think. What better way to act than to give of yourself or your time to help others? Obeying the Law of Gratitude is part of and includes the Law of Attraction.

When you use your thoughts to manifest something in your life, you are in fact telling the universe what you want. You put feelings and emotions into it. You vibrate to it. It becomes a part of you. Every ounce of your very being is tuned into it. Now, to complete the cycle of energy flow, you must complete the circuit by allowing the results to occur for you. You must intent it to come to you unrestricted. This is why some people seem to get what they want while others do not.

The people, who do get what they want, use all the Laws of the Universe in precisely the right way. They are not only tuned into their own thoughts and feelings, but they feel it in their soul. They vibrate to it and they acknowledge it as already being a part of them. They send out the signal to the universe that they are one with what they want and are claiming that they are allowing themselves to receive it without doubt, fear, or worry. This, my friends, is what you need to do if you want to get what you want.

The Law of Allowing will work for you if you let it. What you must agree on is that you are worthy to receive your gift. That you are worthy to receive the prize you are after. The problem with this world is that people are constantly pushing things away. What they don't seem to realize is that the Law of Attraction states that what you think about or wish for you will receive. If you think about war, you'll see more war. If you think about drugs, you'll see more drugs. The fact is, you are allowing these things into your life, and this is why you are seeing it.

No wonder people are constantly complaining that they don't have anything. They can't make ends meet. They can't get ahead in life. They can't do this. They can't do that. For every can't there is another creation that is born. If you say you can't afford this because you don't have enough money, you are telling the universe in fact that you don't have any money. Well guess what? The universe hears you and obeys. Your wish is my command and you get what you wish for. You are allowing poverty in your life and this is why you don't have abundance.

So how can you change this? How can you reverse this and become more abundant in your life? Simple. Just intent it. You have to think about what you want, not what you don't want. If you wish for more money, intent it. Don't go around saying you can't afford something. You are telling the universe that you can't afford it. Therefore, you won't get the money you want. But if you switch that around and tell the universe that you do want it, that you do have the money, the universe will respond and give it to you. It is that simple.

The bottom line here is that you must remember to use all the Laws of the Universe if you expect to get what you want. You must complete the cycle of energy in order to complete the circuit between you and the universe. You are the power source and the universe is the component part of the circuit. The path will flow but it will stop with the universe if you do not have a complete path for the energy to return. This means you must use the Law of Allowing to accept what you wish for. This will complete the path back to you and you will receive what you wished for. You in fact, sent your energy to the component, and the component responded by turning on. It then sent the energy back to you to complete the circuit and to tell you everything is working on all cylinders.

This is the way the Law of Allowing works. If you work in harmony with it, focus your energy the right way, and tell the universe you want it and are ready to receive it, you will get it.

The best way to practice the Law of Allowing is by simply saying "yes" to things you receive in your life. If someone says something nice to you, say "thanks." You are telling the person you are allowing his comments to be received. If someone gives you a gift, say "thanks." You are telling the universe and the person that you are allowing yourself to receive the gift. You need to do this with everything in life that you want to receive. Of course, if you don't want something, you politely say "no" to it. But be careful here. What you say "no" to may benefit you in the long run later. So be sure that you think about it before you say "no." In one form or fashion, you just may need that situation or product or whatever it is you are saying "no" to.

To fully understand the Law of Allowing, you have to look at it from the standpoint of resistance. If you resist something, you will not get it. That is as simple an explanation as you can have. When you use the Law of Allowing, you are saying that you have no resistance to what you want and the flow of energy will be easy and direct. There will be no stumbling blocks.

Your thoughts control your actions. Your thoughts dictate what you end up getting from the Universe. If you believe completely that you will receive what you wish for, good things will come your way.

You must accept that which you wish upon. You must be tuned into the universe to get it. You must be in vibration to what you want. You must show the universe you want it by having gratitude for what you have received. You also must show that you are allowing it by being receptive to it and saying "yes" to it when it comes. By doing this, the universe will manifest it to reality and provide you more.

You simply have to start the process with a thought, turn that thought in an image, send it to your heart for processing (this turns into emotions and feelings), act on your thoughts, and allow the results to come to you. By doing this you will receive results from your thoughts, whether they are good or bad.

The old saying is, "be careful what you wish for" or "you are your thoughts" holds true here in every respect. Therefore, watch your thoughts if you want the best that life has to offer.

FOURTEEN - Listen To What The Universe Is Telling You

ARE you paying attention to what the universe is trying to say to you? You need to recognize that you are surrounded by its vast, immeasurable power. All you need to do is align yourself with the universe. To do this, you have to be more attentive to its messages.

What kind of messages, you ask? These are often the things we take for granted, like coincidences or a flash of insight. Coincidences are a perfect example of a message from the universe. They usually have a message, if we would probe further. Coincidences are one way the universe gives us what we want. For example, you may be visualizing driving your dream car. A few days later, you run into an acquaintance you have not seen for years. You start talking and later you will not be able to exactly recall how it happened but you find out that he knows someone who is selling your dream car at a discounted price. You go that person and sure enough, it looks exactly like your dream car. It is your dream car.

What do you think would have happened if you just said hi to your acquaintance and went on your way? You would have missed that perfect "coincidence." So, stay alert for these things.

In truth, there are no coincidences. Everything happens for a reason. If you declare your intention of wanting something, the universe will bring people, circumstances and events your way to make it happen so long as you are specific, accepting and faithful that it will materialize.

Watch out for the following in particular:

1. Something that suddenly pops into your mind. Are there instances where a person, a place or anything else suddenly - and persistently - crosses your mind? Talk to that person. Go to that place. It might just be the key to your dreams.

2. Something that suddenly jumps out to you. You are walking in a bookstore or library and suddenly a book catches your attention. You do not know why - it just jumped out from the background from all the other hundreds of books there.

Read it. There is most likely a message there for you.

3. Sudden urges. You are on your way home and you have a sudden, unexplainable urge to take a different route. Take that route. You will probably find some surprises along the way.

Of course, these sudden urges should not be confused with impulses, especially buying impulses, like the urge of wanting to buy that dress or that gadget. You know why you want these things. Sudden urges from the universe do not usually have a logical reason behind them.

4. Frequent or sudden contact with certain people. Have you ever been in a seminar or any gathering where you find yourself making unintentional eye contact with a person there three times or more?

Or have you experienced seeing one person three times in one day in very different places?

Or, like the example given above, have you met a friend or someone you know whom you have not seen in a long time?

Talk to these people. Again, they may just bring you closer to your dream.

An exception, though, would be if you are attracted to the person and think of them regularly or constantly. Naturally, the universe will find ways for you to see that person. So your meeting is a result of your thinking and visualization, and not a bridge for what you want to materialize.

5. Dreams. Have you ever had a very vivid, recurring dream? Though interpreting dreams can be tricky and may require the analysis of an expert, you can make an attempt at analyzing your dream by asking yourself the following questions:

"How do I feel about this?"

"How would this compare in general to my life right now?

"Is this parallel to any event happening to me right now or one that will happen?"

Your sleeping dreams may not only show you the way to your waking dreams but may also be able to show you if you still have any blocks in your subconscious, such as doubt, fear or low self-esteem.

Generally, you are trying to develop your intuition here. Over time, it will be easier for you to watch out for any messages from the universe.

Be careful, though, that you do not mistake intuition for an impulse. While intuition usually springs from calm, impulse springs from a burst of desire, fear or desperation. To distinguish intuition from impulse, intuition consultant and trainer Nancy Rosanoff advises following what she states as the Universal Law of Three. She said that if a thought comes back to her three times, she does it. Intuitive thoughts and feelings are "insistent and persistent."

So you do not have to act immediately, especially in situations where something is at stake for you. In some cases, though, you have to act immediately, as with the example given earlier - when you suddenly meet an acquaintance. You have nothing to lose in that situation so go ahead and act. It is big decisions like making an investment or choosing a partner that requires the application of the Universal Law of Three.

Continue to be alert for messages from the universe. Eventually, it will become second nature to you.

Positive energy = power. So the more positive you are, the more powerful your thoughts are!

So how do you keep the positive fire burning, day in, day out? Here are some tips:

1. Find something to be grateful for everyday. Every morning, when you wake up, be thankful for another day. Thank the universe for another opportunity to enjoy life, for a chance to achieve the things you want.

Remember the earlier exercise of making a list of the things you are grateful for? You can review your list every morning upon waking and every night before going to bed. Or, every day you can point to an item there at random and express your thanks for it. During the day, you can also look for something to be grateful for, however small or big it is. It could be a call from a friend, a compliment from an officemate, a hug from a loved one and so on.

2. Refresh yourself in your sanctuary. Close your eyes, breathe deeply and relax. Picture your ideal place, a beautiful place where you feel safe, calm and relaxed. See the sights, hear the sounds, feel the feelings of actually being there.

It can be by the beach, with sparkling blue waves and pristine white powdery sand, with a fresh breeze blowing through your hair and the waves crashing against your feet. Or it can be in a meadow full of flowers bursting abloom in different colors, with brilliant butterflies and dragonflies flying from flower to flower.

Whatever that place is, it should be a place of rest for you. Stay in that place for a while until you feel light and energized. Visit that place regularly, especially when you feel stressed.

3. Affirm daily. The affirmation may not be specifically related to your goal, but a declaration of the good things in life in general like "Life is beautiful" or "Everyday is wonderful and full of surprises." You can also boost your mind power and state of mind by affirming: "I can get everything I want if I ask" or "I am building the life I want."

4. Look for the positive in every situation. Good or bad, know that there is always something good – and maybe even a golden opportunity – in every situation. Again, remember that there are no coincidences. Remember that everything happens for a good reason. So when your plans are cancelled or have to be changed at the last minute, don't fret. There might be something else meant for you to do that day. Pay attention to the signs the universe will give you.

Should you have a hard time finding anything good in a bad situation, let go of the negative feelings you have as soon as you can. Remember that negative creates more negative, so do not dwell on it. Instead, focus all your energy on the positive.

5. Read motivational articles or books daily. Make this a habit, even if only for a few minutes every day. The advice in these articles and books will not only give you ideas on how to reach your goal, it will also put you in

a positive state of mind. And reading them every day will give you that positive feeling every day too.

However, if positive media can have a powerful impact, negative media can also do the same. This is particularly damaging if it lingers in your mind even after you have been exposed to it. And even if it does not, it can reach your subconscious. So if you keep watching a soap opera depicting poverty, for example, how do you think it will affect your mind power? Or your belief in the abundance of the universe?

So choose the shows you watch, the books and magazines you read, the websites you visit and any other media, more carefully. In case you still absorb a negative message – for example, you read about an accident in the newspaper – make sure it is not the first thing you see in the morning or the last thing you see at night. What begins and what ends your day should always be positive.

Music is also very powerful, arguably more so than words. Though you may like sentimental music, be sure that you also include happy, lively tunes for your ears regularly.

6. Lift others up. If you give energy, you get more energy. (Giving is discussed in detail in the next magical tip). Pay someone a compliment, listen to a friend in need, comfort a loved one, or simply smile.

Do you know that you can bless another person? Yes, not only when you say "Bless you" to a person when they sneeze. When you wish another person well, especially if you are saying it to that person directly, you are sending them positive energy.

Making others feel good can automatically make you feel good.

These tips may be hard to apply at first, but once you get used to doing them for some time, you will be surprised at how they will eventually become second nature to you. Aim to be positive daily for 21 days, and it will be easier for you afterwards. Doing something 21 times makes it a habit.

And once being positive is second nature to you, so will the manifestation of your dreams.

The same principle applies to your thoughts. Hold them close to you, but not so tightly that they are "suffocated" and are never realized. Give them enough freedom to "fly" out to the universe. Holding on to your thoughts and dreams too tightly might be a sign of doubt or fear on your part. As mentioned in one of the magical tips, you have to believe - really believe - that your thoughts will materialize. Having this attitude will help you take a relaxed attitude towards your dreams - after all, you know they will come true!

Another reason why you should not be too fixated on your thoughts is that there might be something better the universe can give you. As mentioned in one of the magical tips, the universe has its own power. And it can actually give you something even better than what you originally asked for. So, when phrasing affirmations, always give room for something better (e.g. I am now happily earning a [amount] salary or even higher.). Be open to receiving more than what you asked for.

Consciousness teacher and writer Shakti Gawain, in her book "Creative Visualization," aptly describes the feeling of letting go and yet taking control at the same time:

Let us imagine that life is a river. Most people are clinging to the bank, afraid to let go and risk being carried along by the current of the river. At a certain point, each person must be willing to simply let go, and trust the river to carry him or her along safely. At this point he learns to "go with the flow" and it feels wonderful.

Once he has gotten used to being in the flow of the river, he can begin to look ahead and guide his own course onward, deciding where the course looks best, steering his way around boulders and snags, and choosing which of the many channels and branches of the river he prefers to follow, all the while still "going with the flow."

So hold on to your goals but not too tightly. Keep your desired outcome very clear in your mind but be open to a different one. The universe may just give you a very pleasant surprise.

So now that you know what you should do, what are you waiting for? Go use that mind power you are now aware of and make your dreams come true! Apply the magical tips you learned!

THE MEDIUMSHIP OF SPIRIT

If you are not that confident yet or if you would like to put the magical tips here to the test first, you can start small. For example, you may visualize seeing and talking with a particular person. Or eating a particular food. Or hailing a cab, especially in areas with many people waiting for one. Put the magic to the test – and marvel at the results.

For as long as you are clear and specific with an image in your mind and with all the faith in your heart, you will get what you asked for.

And in case you do not get it the first time you asked, do not be discouraged. Try and try again! Mind power can be compared with a special skill like playing an instrument or taking up a course in college. You learn it. And you need to practice it as often as you can to really get it.

In case what you want does not materialize, you can ask yourself, based on the earlier magical tips, what exactly is stopping you from achieving your goal. Review your thoughts and feelings at the time you set your goal and visualized it. Did you have any doubts, even the slightest, that it will happen? Did you fear that you were not going to get it? Or even – are you afraid of possible negative consequences once you achieve your goal? Concentrate and try to get to the root.

Be sensitive to your feelings. If you feel anything negative after setting a goal, ask yourself why. If you identify the reason, you can face it head-on. If it is just doubt, guilt or any of the blocks mentioned previously, just review your affirmations and do the exercises in the magical tips.

To help you master your mind power, keep a notebook where you write each time you succeed in applying it. No matter how big or small, record each success you have in your notebook. It will give you assurance that indeed your mind power does work especially when you feel low in energy or are suddenly doubtful. And remember, the universe is a very huge, very potent and very giving source of power. Trust that even the smallest effort on your part can generate massive results because you are riding on the power of the universe.

Visualization is an important aspect to mastering your mind power and the Law of Attraction. Some people, however, feel that it is not quite proper to visualize for things. "It's too material" they say. But material form is necessary for the self-recognition of spirit from the individual standpoint. And this is the means through which the creative process is carried forward. Therefore, far from matter being an illusion and something that ought not to be (as some metaphysical teachers have taught), matter is the necessary channel for the self-differentiation of spirit.

We all possess more power and greater possibilities than we realize, and visualizing is one of the greatest of these powers. It brings other possibilities to our observation. When we pause to think for a moment, we realize that for a cosmos to exist at all, it must be the outcome of a cosmic mind, which binds all individual minds to a certain generic unities of action, thereby producing all things as realities and nothing as illusions.

If you consider matter in its right order as the polar opposite to Spirit, you will not find any antagonism between them. On the contrary, together they constitute one harmonious whole. And when you realize this you feel, in your practice of visualizing, that you are working from cause to effect, from beginning to finish. In reality your mental picture is the specialized working of the originating spirit.

The same power that brought universal substance into existence will bring your individual thought or mental picture into physical form. There is no difference of kind in the power. The only difference is a difference of scale. The power and the substance themselves are the same. Only in working out your mental picture it has transferred its creative energy from the universal to the scale of the particular, and is working in the same unfailing manner from its specific center, your mind.

There is nothing unusual or mysterious in the idea of your pictured desire coming into material evidence. It is the working of a universal natural Law. The world was projected by the self-contemplation of the Universal Mind, and this same action is taking place in its individualized branch which is the Mind of Man. Everything in the whole world has its beginning in mind and comes into existence in exactly the same manner from the hat on your head to the boots on your feet. All are projected thoughts, solidified.

Your personal advance in evolution depends upon your right use of the power of visualizing, and your use of it depends on whether you recognize that you, yourself, are a particular center through and in which the originating spirit is finding ever new expression for potentialities already existing within itself. This is evolution; this continual unfolding of existing though outwardly invisible things.

Your mental picture is the force of attraction that evolves and combines the originating substance into specific shape. Your picture is the combining and evolving powerhouse, so to speak, through which the originating Creative Spirit expressed itself. Its creative action is limitless, without beginning and without end, and always progressive and orderly. It proceeds stage by stage, each stage being a necessary preparation for the one to follow.

By saturating your mind with vivid representations of you living your dream life, you inescapably communicate the goal to your subconscious mind. Your subconscious will start to work on your "target" within a few days of starting your visualization practice. The more you visualize, the quicker you'll "attract" your goals. And the more your subconscious understands what you want, the more effortless the whole process will seem.

When you visualize, you invariably go to a "higher level of vibration." You feel more confident, self-assured, motivated & committed. This is because when you visualize you actually "vibrate" at the level you would if you had actually achieved your goals. The very act of Visualization creates the very "vibrations" you need to shift your results. Plus, it's easier to maintain this energy in a quiet room when you visualize, as opposed to being at work surrounded by negative people, for example.

So let's break this down to five steps:

1. Know your end goal and visualize in first person mode. Hear, smell, touch and see it. Do this for 5-10 minutes when drifting to sleep at night.

2. Feel good while visualizing. One good way is to listen to emotional music that will resonate with what you are trying to manifest. I try to imagine the music is "playing for your moment of glory" which is your manifestation. This can be an excellent way to feel the emotions associated with your desire.

3. Think about your end goal from time to time throughout the day. Do not look for it just know it's coming.

4. Do not worry about how you will get to your end goal. Instead do whatever action you feel will bring you closer to it. Just know by visualizing and working towards the goal it will happen.

5. Have faith your end goal has manifested and expect it. Belief is very powerful and the best way to build belief is to start manifesting small items like quarters etc. Something you know could happen even without the Law of Attraction. But the key here is once you start manifesting specific small common items your belief in the Law of Attraction will rise and you can move on to larger items.

Now I think one of the main keys here is to be as emotional as possible while visualizing. You need to feel good while seeing your end goal in your mind. I really think this is one of the keys which effects the speed of manifestation. I think this and belief are very important.

Other Things That Can Help:

Determine your end goals. This is really important and even I struggle with this. It can be hard to pin point exactly what you want and how it will look once manifested. I think this especially relates to careers and events more so than objects.

Write down your end goals in a journal. Know the very act of writing them down is giving power to manifesting your end goal. Read your journal whenever you feel inspired to.

Look at yourself in the mirror and repeat your end goals as if they have manifested already. Then just say something at the end like "this has happened! I have total faith in the law. Thank you!"

Act as if your manifestation has already happened. If you want to manifest a cruise you need to start getting your clothes together, check the weather for the cruise, see if the ship allows you to bring food on it etc.

If you follow these tips with a strong belief you will see your manifestations happen. Just remember to have faith even if you have not seen your manifestation appear right away.

FIFTEEN: Five Great Secrets

ORGANIZED religion today tries to convince their followers that God the Creator only speaks to the Priests and Ministers. They insist that their followers should only believe what their Ministers tell them, since God the Creator has no time to talk to the rest of his flock. This is the great lie that has been passed down to us for generations.

God talks to us all, everyday. You do not need a Minister to act as an interpreter for God. God's greatest desire is for all of us to be happy and prosperous and to live our lives as was his intention during the Golden age of Mankind.

Our world and the world of Spirit are connected by unseen bonds of mystic energies that all of us can tap into to bring joy and happiness into our lives. This is available to anyone who is willing to cast aside the negative aspects of the modern world and accept help from the astral worlds.

Your spirit guides, Angels, and the Ascended Masters are waiting right now to bring the great wisdom of God the Creator to planet Earth and usher back the Golden Age of Mankind that has eluded us for so long. The only question you have to ask yourself is are you truly ready to learn the simple answers to an uncomplicated Universe?

Your reality is a unique manifestation of God the Creator. God created your reality so that it may explore itself within the illusion of being separate from itself. The reality around you is a complete mirror of what you are, and what you are is God. Or to put it another way, you are an individualization manifestation of God that has entered the illusion that you are separate from God.

The other people that share your reality with you are also you (God) and yet in this reality you have the ability to see them and say 'They are not me.' This is made possible by the mechanism of your reality, which grants you total freewill. At the soul level you choose what you experience.

Understanding that your freewill is total can be hard to believe from within your reality. You are blinded to the fact that you are the master of your reality and select every experience that you have.

Your freewill is so powerful that it can choose to give away its power. Your reality is so powerful that God can enter it and cease to know it is God. It can even be surrounded by all that it is and still not see itself. This power comes from the beauty of the mechanism through which your reality is formed.

From one perspective your reality is a mechanism, a blueprint, a set of rules. When we speak of it in this respect we wish to convey the perspective from which the mechanism of your universe is without consciousness. We are 'zooming in' if you like on the pure relationship between you and the reality you experience.

The mechanism through which your reality is created is incredibly pure and simple. At any place in time you are what we will call a vibration. This vibration is a form of energy signature that you continually radiate. This frequency of this vibration is determined by your belief system, which is basically that which you believe to be true.

As you move through different sensations and states of being you send out the energy of your vibration. To this the mechanism of your reality says only one thing to you. It says, "And So It Is". Whenever you feel 'Oh this is fabulous!' you send out that energy. Whenever you feel 'This is a disaster, everything is falling apart!' you send out that energy. The universe does not in any way analyze or contemplate this. It does not think before it sends you a reply. It simply takes what you send out and reflects it back to you, saying 'And So It Is'.

SECRETS OF THE UNIVERSE

Connection to, and application of each one of these secrets is connection to power. All which requires our awareness is manifested and resolved through these.

The Secret of Reality: Our physical world is a dream world, and it works just like dreaming. As you acknowledge this reality and work with it from that perspective, the apparent speed of action increases. The way to direct the world is through your imagination and will. Exercising your will strengthens it. You can exercise it by doing something unpleasant until it becomes pleasant.

THE MEDIUMSHIP OF SPIRIT

The Secret of Creation: The flow and magnification of energy is directed both consciously and unconsciously by thoughts, feelings and emotions and this creates one's reality. Energy flows and builds to wherever one directs it. We are the power that creates reality.

The Secret of Love: Love is the essence, the glue and the fabric of all that is and is the energy that moves through all. Love heals and restores all. Loving your neighbor is loving God. Forgiving your neighbor is forgiving God. When you see a lack of God's love or grace in any condition – look again.

The Secret of Truth: Truth exists in everything as the higher awareness of God the Creator. Truth rises to the surface of all situations as one loves all karmic creations free. Truth is received as higher learning, realizations.

The Secret of Life: We are infinite beings pretending to be finite. We have created forms and conditions to escape the limitations of formlessness. The key to mastery is to acknowledge reality. Reality is a simulation. The future pours into the past thru the funnel of your thinking. Change what you are thinking now, and the future will take care of itself.

Life in this three-dimensional existence has made us forget many spiritual truths. Karma exists and operates only in the present moment. It is your beliefs, decisions, and actions today about yourself and the world around you that give you what you have and make you what you are. Thanks to memory we may carry over habits of body and mind from day to day, but each day is a new creation and any habit can be changed at any present moment, even if it isn't easy.

Many people living today are not even here; most of their attention is focused on the past or the future. To the degree they diminish their awareness of the present moment, their power and effectiveness in the present also decreases. Human consciousness is sufficiently subtle to impact the Natural Laws that uphold the progression of the Universe.

What we get in our lives is what our thoughts, emotions and intentions bring to us. All are asked to take responsibility for all manifested reflections in walking one's return journey home.

THE MEDIUMSHIP OF SPIRIT

BOOKS BY WILLIAM ALEXANDER ORIBELLO
PUBLISHED BY INNER LIGHT PUBLICATIONS
AVAILABLE FROM AMAZON.COM
OR, TIMOTHY G BECKLEY
BOX 753,
NEW BRUNSWICK, NJ 08903

Bible Spells

Candle Burning Magic With The Psalms

Godspells

Sacred Magic

The Sealed Magical Book Of Moses

Candle Burning To Contact Your Guardian Angel

Master Book Of Spiritual Power

Cosmic Secrets Of The Masters Of Wisdom

Divine Bible Spells

Para-X Powers (partial)

Curses And Their Reverses (partial)

Count Saint Germain The Prophet Who Lives Forever

Angels Of The Lord - Expanded Edition (partial)

DVDs

Get Rich Quick Money Spells

Secrets Signs And Symbols to Contact Count Saint Germain

5 Easy Steps To Psychic Self Defense

Books are $20 each - DVDs $22 each
Add ships of $5 for up to 3 items - $8 for 4 items or more

THE MEDIUMSHIP OF SPIRIT

If you enjoyed this book, please write for our free catalog.

Global Communications
PO Box 753
New Brunswick, NJ 08903

Or, send us an e-mail: mrufo8@hotmail.com

www.conspiracyjournal.com

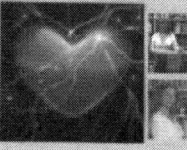

35872894R00070

Made in the USA
Lexington, KY
27 September 2014